"CUSTOMER PERCEPTION OF SERVICE QUALITY IN HOTEL INDUSTRY": A

BY - MS. MALINI SINGH

CONTENTS

ABSTRACT

The study on **"Customer perception of Service Quality in Hotel Industry": A case study in Bangalore** provides empirical study towards solving the challenge for the hotel management to determine the satisfaction level of their most important service quality dimensions so as to improve on them and ultimately improve on their service quality levels. This will enable the hotel owners to retain existing customers and attract new ones at a lower cost.

The quality of service in hotel industry is an important factor of successful business. The existing trend of complete quality management in hotel industry ensures the achievement of competitive advantage of hotel companies and is therefore the subject of contemporary research into service quality in hotel industry. High customer satisfaction is critically important to the hotel industry; therefore, the importance and performance of Hotel should be examined from guests' perspectives. The quality of product and service in hotel industry is an important factor of successful business. This study examines customers' perception of Hotel product and service. The success of the hotel and lodging industry in a global environment depends on its degree of professionalism. Product quality and service efficiency need to be strengthened if a more professional lodging work force is to emerge. Delivering quality product and service is an essential strategy for success and survival in today's competitive environment. For this study five renowned star hotel of Bangalore have been surveyed and studied and analysis has been done. The research has been done to help hotels to improve their product on the whole so necessary a recommendation has also been given.

The concept and the conceptual model of service quality is indispensable if we wish to understand the genesis of service quality and potential gaps in quality. The aim of this thesis is to show the importance of service quality in hotel industry from both the conceptual standpoint and that of service quality measurement. The thesis describes the most common criteria for measuring service quality, namely the model of internal service quality and the SERVQUAL model. The shown results are those of quantitative and qualitative application of such models in hotels.

This study is based on comparison of service quality of star hotels in Bangalore. The study highlights the customer expectation of Hotel as a product and also reveals the gap between the tangibles expected by the guest and the tangibles provided by the hotel.

The purpose of this study was to examine and describe hotel guests' perception of service quality in relation to services offered by the hotels. This study investigated how to improve service quality through service satisfaction survey. The significance of this study was that the finding would encourage hotel management to improve and develop their service and product and also focus training program towards better guest seervice.

INDEX

CHAPTER 1.1 (A)

INTRODUCTION

In the hospitality industry quality is one of the competitive priorities which enable hotels to survive. Providing excellent service quality and high customer satisfaction is the most important issue and challenge facing the contemporary service industry (Hung, Huang. and Chen, 2003). Service quality has for long been recognized to play a critical role in a firm's success. Quality is understood to mean conformance to specifications, though more recently it is taken to mean meeting and /or exceeding customers' expectations. Kandampully, Mok and Sparks (2001) suggested that attempt to have effective service quality management is the best way to achieve superior customer satisfaction.

Oakland (2005) and Kandampully, et al., (2001) showed that service quality can only be achieved if organizations empower their employees to underpin service quality dimensions. These dimensions include tangibles (physical facilities, equipments, and appearance of personnel); reliability (ability to perform the promised service dependably and accurately); responsiveness (willingness to help customers and provide prompt service); assurance (knowledge and courtesy of employees and their ability to convey trust and confidence); and empathy (caring, individualized attention provided to customers).

In the hospitality industry, communicating service quality begins with an understanding of the aspects of service quality that are most important to customers. Pariseau and McDaniel (1997) stressed that in order to attract customers, a firm has to serve their needs and retain them. Failure to achieve this may yield customer complaints, lack of repeat purchase and loss of customer loyalty. The ultimate result of this is low competitiveness of the firm, yet today's survival in the market place is guaranteed by a firm's ability to outpace its competition. Although service quality management has been embraced world over in the hospitality industry, many hotels in Bangalore city have not embraced the concept fully. Surveys of the hotels within Bangalore city and other hotels outside the city in India revealed that the degree to which management has defined quality, empowered employees to deliver quality is not clear. There are service quality inefficiencies in terms of low grade tangibles such as utensils, beds, room size, etc. These have led to limited customer assurance, low reliability, responsiveness and empathy which have cost the organizations sums of money as a result of low repeat purchases. For most of the hotels, the processes through which bills are made, food is delivered, and the ways bookings are confirmed are all slow. Yet these facilities endeavor in every possible way to achieve superior customer satisfaction growth over the last five years. Management of these hotels does not seem to have a specific way of measuring quality and its general perception of service quality dimensions seems less than standard. Customer complaints are enormous and efforts to rectify them are usually reactive rather than proactive. The net result is that customer satisfaction is low in the hotels.

Overview

Tourism is not just about the facilities and attractions provided for visitors. It is about people and especially about the relationship between the customer and the individual and organization providing service. Everybody employed in tourism needs to have the knowledge, skills and attitudes to provide high standard of product and service that customers expect. The single largest trend in business in India over the past sixty years has been the increased emphasis on service and service-related industries. Service has not traditionally been viewed as being as important as manufacturing. But service is no longer merely a by-product of an industrial society. According to Davidoff, many companies start to be engaged in efforts to improve the quality of service to their customers. However, improving service quality has not received the same attention and favor as has improving manufacturing quality. This is probably true because it is much harder to quantify and judge service. Davidoff mentioned, "Service grows on its own strength, as more people require its products independent of manufacturing. The number of well-paying service jobs continues to grow. The numerous and high productivity service jobs require highly skilled and trained workers with a variety of opportunity for advancement."

RESEARCH CONTEXT

The service-based lodging industry's goal is 100 % guest satisfaction. In India, number of approved hotels by the government of India as on 31st Dec 2010 is 2483 and number of salable Rooms is 117815. (Govt. of India tourism survey 2010). Even in Karnataka, there are more than 80 approved Hotels with at least 15 competitors, which guarantee 100 % guest satisfaction and which have higher average occupancy.

Because the hospitality industry is a service-oriented industry, poor customer service will cause a low occupancy rate. Generally, customers will remember negative experiences twice as often as positive ones. (1999, Feiertag) Therefore, to survive in this high competitive industry, hotels have to consider how to give better customer service than other competitors.

Evans (1998) discussed about poor customer service and worst customer satisfaction in the hotel industry. She stated that the hotel industry scored 71 out of 100 points in the industry's best-known customer satisfaction survey, compared with drop from 75 points in 1994 when lodging companies were struggling to pull themselves out of a recession. The year of 1998's score was the lowest since Andersen began its American customer satisfaction index five years ago. The survey found that guests don't believe hotels are providing services that justify the rising room costs, giving the hotels a score of 73 in this category, the lowest in five years. Nearly one-quarter of the consumers surveyed said that hotel guests had voiced complaints over such things as sloppy housekeeping, time-consuming check-outs and tardy room service. As time progresses, hotel's room rate continued to increase but customer service is still more and more poor.

In recent decades, significant growth in the hospitality industry has been fueled by increases in disposable income, leisure time, and political stability. Many third world countries turn to hospitality and tourism as an economic development strategy shortly after achieving political stability. Aggressive tourism campaigns have also fueled the hospitality industry's growth (Kirwin, 1991). Consequently, the hospitality industry has grown both larger and more competitive; and organizations in the hospitality industry face increasing competitive pressures. Because of this growth, service quality also takes on increasing importance both domestically and internationally in hospitality business environment that face tremendous competition and rapid deregulation. This results in a need for hotels to serve an increasingly diverse clientele that includes customers who have backgrounds and cultural expectations that reflect a wide range of experience with industrialization and globalization.

For truly global products, uniformity can drive down research, engineering, design, and production costs across business functions, contributing to a cycle of higher global competition. Multinational companies that pursue strategies of product adaptation frequently run the risk of falling victim to global competitors that have recognized opportunities to serve global customers (Keegan & Green, 2000). To successfully compete in this dynamic environment, many hospitality companies both domestically and internationally are focusing on improving service quality. High service quality is a strategy that has been related to success especially during times of intense competition both domestically and internationally (Wong, Dean, & White, 1999). Service quality is a very important factor for achieving competitive advantages and efficiency. For example, hotel businesses must seek profitable ways to differentiate their services/products from other lodging companies. Service attributes, such as imprecise standards and fluctuating demand, have been identified. Those attributes further complicate the task of defining, delivering, and measuring service quality in the hospitality industry (Wong, Dean, & White, 1999). To increase their competitive advantage over other lodging companies, hoteliers must deliver each and every service related sector with high service quality to optimize customer satisfaction. Oliver (1981) defined customer satisfaction as a customer's emotional response to the use of a product or service. Measuring customer satisfaction is an integral part of the effort to improve a product's quality, expecting to result in repeat purchases and favorable word-of-mouth publicity, and, ultimately, a company's competitive advantage. Service satisfaction is a function of the service setting and the consumers' experiences and reactions to a provider's behavior during the service encounter period. Several work environmental situations within each hotel service sector can create gaps in services as well as result in hotel employee stress (Hardin, 2002).

Gone are the days when quality meant neat bed, good food and clean bathrooms. The definition of quality in today's day has drastically complicated and the level of service has surpassed all milestones. Quality is one of the competitive priorities which enable firms in the hospitality industry to survive. Providing excellent service quality and high customer satisfaction is the most important issue and challenge facing the contemporary service industry (Hung, Huang. and Chen, 2003). Service quality has for long been recognized to play a critical role in a firm's competitive advantage (Fitzsimmons and Fitzsimmons, 1994). Quality is understood to mean conformance to specifications, though more recently it is taken to mean meeting and /or exceeding customers' expectations. Kandampully, Mok and Sparks (2001) suggested that attempt to have effective service quality management is the best way to achieve superior customer satisfaction.

Today's Hospitality customer

Given below are the outlooks of the changing customer. The customers today are:

- Health and wellness conscious
- Have more disposable income
- Green/environment friendly and socially aware
- Perspective and judgmental about a brand
- Often use holidays for connecting with family
- Work hard and rest too hard
- Experimental and adventures
- More exotic
- Look for something different

AIM AND SCOPE OF THE STUDY

The study on **"Customer perception of Service Quality in Hotel Industry": A case study of Bangalore** provides empirical study towards solving the challenge for the hotel management to determine the satisfaction level of service quality dimensions and to improve their service quality levels. This will enable the hotel owners to retain existing customers and attract new ones at a lower cost.

Before we get into the detail study we need to look at the overall picture of the hospitality industry in India. We also need to understand the Bangalore Hotel market to justify our study

Bangalore Hotel Market - an Overview

For Bangalore's hotel and tourism industries prospects remain positive in the coming years, with more than 7,794 hotel rooms expected to be added in the next couple of years, including international hotels, offerings from the Ritz-Carlton, Shangri-La and J.W Marriott.

In view of the substantial planned room additions, occupancies are forecasted to stabilize around 65-70 % in the next 5 years with daily room rate averaging at Rs.16, 000.

The tourism industry in Bangalore, which receives more business travelers than leisure tourists both from the international and domestic markets, is set for further growth by improvements made to the tourism infrastructure and the continued growth of inbound arrivals.

Given its strategic location as a key gateway, particularly for domestic tourists, to the World Heritage sites and historical locations in the State, Bangalore is in a good position to further expand its leisure tourism potential.

Besides, the city is also aiming to become a healthcare hub by 2013, with heavy investments by the Manipal Group, Wockhardt and Columbia Asia to increase the number of hospital beds in the city.

Bangalore is leading the recovery in the domestic hotel industry. In the garden city, the rate of recovery was faster in the first half of the year compared to other business destinations like Mumbai and Delhi.

It has seen occupancy rates improving on a month-on-month basis, with February reporting the highest occupancy rate at 80% and average room rates touching close to the levels of early 2009 at Rs. 10,136.

Source: Business line, Oct 2011

The above data reflects the growth of hospitality industry in Bangalore. A study on service quality on Bangalore hotels will help hotels to sustain the demand of the hotel and offer excellent quality service to both domestic and international traveler

Common problems faced by star hotel guests in Bangalore

The guests in hotels face a wide range of problems because of poor service and product of the hotel. Below are mentioned a few of them which are most common

- Time taking services
- Overall cleanliness of the hotel
- Security of the hotel
- No booking on arrival
- Non-responsive staff
- Uncomfortable rooms and amenities
- Noisy surrounding
- Overcharged
- Poor room service
- Overpriced services
- Sub Standard restaurant food and service

- Inaccurate star rating
- Retention charges

It is to be noticed that most of the problems mentioned above are related to service quality. This has motivated the researcher to take a study on service quality in star hotels in Bangalore which will play a key role in effective quality management of hotel industry. The study will also help hotels to understand the problems faced by their guest and overcome them.

The study also reveals the importance of training in Hotel Industry. In this highly competitive lodging industry, each company must analyze and consider their training program. Good training will benefit the entire organization. Training reduces tensions, turnover, and cost and improves product and quality of service. (Shriver, 1988 & Tanke, 1990) Customer count is certainly going to improve the company image and the bottom line. Now many companies in the hospitality recognize training and have developed systematic training program. However, not everyone in this industry sees training as an investment. Many managers of small operations consider training as an exercise in futility because they believe it takes more time than it is worth, employee do not stay long enough for it to pay, people are not interested in being trained, and the like. Also people in entry-level service jobs tend to think, they should be able to do these jobs without training. So in fact, it is hard to convince these people that training is worth investment. It is difficult to measure and prove the difference training makes because there are always many variables in every situation. One way to reassure whether training pays off is to compare individual operations where the training is good with those that do little or no training. The differences will be obvious in "atmosphere," in "smoothness of operation," in "customer's satisfaction in improved quality of service." (Miller, 1998)

Davidoff (1994) stated that once an educated person gets into the workforce, there is little training in service available. Even though service companies provide a training program, most of the training concentrates on the technical aspects of the job. They neglect the significant real intangible service training. What separates one hotel from another is the quality of service. It is what people remember. (Rowe, 1998)

Davidoff suggested one of the things it takes for service to succeed is training system and education. He said the major reason why service is so bad today involved the lack of proper education and training. To make matters worse, most of businesses are not well prepared to provide the necessary training when a potentially good employee comes out of the education system. Indian companies must remember that a few days and rupees of training will more than pay for itself in the long run. Education and training are an essential part of the modern organization's efforts to support customer-contact personnel in hospitality industry.

Without general education on customer service, employees cannot possibly be equipped to handle the rigorous regular interchange with customers. Without specific training on the processes involved with a particular company and its products, even the most talented service provider will sometimes fall flat on their face. As more and more organization realizes this, the service standard in the hospitality industry will rise. (Davidoff, 1994)

Quality customer service means different things to different people. We cannot assume everyone of employee understands how to provide "quality" customer service the way trainer or executives or human resource intend it to be. It is their responsibility to teach front-line staffs and all customer service providers your company's quality customer service's standards. (Haneborg, 1998)

It is important to invest in continuous quality customer service training for everyone. Organization should provide all employees with continuous education on customer service. Don't stop with one session. If customer service is important to company in the market, company has to be sure staff members attend annual refresher or advance courses, whatever it takes to ensure consistency and quality.

In hospitality industry, achieving outstanding customer service requires much time, energy and money in the customer service training and call center performance and service enhancement areas. (Kelley, 1999) Professional and courteous customer service does not just happen. It requires a company commitment with training extended to all departments and all levels of the company. Training must be an ongoing commitment. Regular and comprehensive measurement of performance and customer attitudes is central to maintaining the commitment.

JUSTIFICATION AND CONTRIBUTIONS OF THE RESEARCH

This research is important for a number of reasons. These include the economic significance of the hotel industry, the paucity of current research and the contribution to both theory and management both in the hotel industry, and the broader service sector, that results from this research. The significance of the industry derives from the economic and employment contributions to the Indian and global economies. There is also a significant indirect contribution to the broader economy. Without the accommodation sector, associated industries such as tourism and the event and conference industries would be unable to operate. Industry generally is also dependent on hotels to support the staff travel necessary for business to operate effectively. As stated previously the hotel industry is a large industry contributing a substantial amount to the Indian and global economies and providing employment for many million people worldwide. In Karnataka only, the broader accommodation industry, that includes motels and serviced apartments as well as hotels, comprises 80 properties with 6408 bedrooms (Indian Bureau of Statistics, 2010) whilst at the global level the hotel industry comprises over seventeen million bedrooms (World Tourism Organisation, 2004 www.world-ourism.org/facts/trends/capacity.htm) in over three hundred thousand hotels (Olsen, 1996). The growth in the hotel industry has reflected the growth in travel patterns, especially those that occurred with the advent of comparatively inexpensive air travel in the latter part of the twentieth century (Weaver & Oh, 1993). This growth is expected to continue with the World Tourism Organisation (2004) forecasting a growth to 1.56 billion international arrivals by the year 2020 from 0.56 billion in 1995 (www.worldtourism. org/facts/trends/capacity.htm). Despite the economic significance of the hotel industry there has been comparatively little previous research that has explored consumer satisfaction in the higher quality segments of the hotel industry. As a result, there are a number of gaps in the literature that this research will address.

Firstly, with the exception of a paper by Wei, Ruys and Muller (1999) that addressed the topic of the gap in perceptions of hotel attributes between marketing managers and older people in Australia, there has been no Indian research found on customer expectations, customer satisfaction or customer service in hotels, or on hotel performance.

Secondly, there is a literature gap in relation to the determinants of customer service in the Chain and Standalone hotel sectors. Even within the broader service industry literature, there is little research that has addressed these particular aspects of the service quality variable in the customer satisfaction.

Thirdly, there is a gap in the literature in respect of the mediating effect of value on the relationships between service quality, and customer satisfaction. Whilst there has been research in the broader service environment on the impact of value there is very limited research in relation to value and value expectations in the hotel industry. The limited volume of previous research enables this research to make a contribution to knowledge and to theory development. This research significantly extends the body of knowledge in relation to a number of the literature gaps mentioned above.

Firstly, there has been very little research conducted in India in respect of hotel satisfaction and, therefore, this research, almost in its entirety, extends the body of knowledge across a number of areas in respect of a geographical extension of research into selection, performance, customer satisfaction and loyalty research within the hotel industry.

Secondly, the relationship between hotel performance and customer satisfaction has not previously been investigated in respect of the Chain and Standalone hotel sectors, and this research will provide greater understanding of the drivers of customer satisfaction in hotels.

This research, therefore, will provide an important contribution to the body of knowledge in this area. And this will also make a practical contribution to management in the hotel industry through empirically sound research that will identify the relationships between performance, and guest satisfaction.

This will be of particular relevance to the global hotel sector that is so reliant on the brand for global marketing strategies (Chon & Sparrowe, 2000; Tepeci, 1999). The hotel industry, in general, will benefit from the increased levels of knowledge and understanding of the factors customers find important in the hotel experience, and of how hotel performance impacts on the levels of satisfaction, and how this, in turn impacts on loyalty intentions. For the Indian hotel industry, this research is mostly groundbreaking as there has been no previous research that has investigated the domestic hotel industry in relation to customer satisfaction. Of particular importance is the need to increase understanding and knowledge relating to consumer behavior and expectations in relation to the Chain and Standalone hotel sectors as the star hotel sectors are less fragmented, and reflect higher levels of concentration, than many of the other hotel sectors (Jones, 2002).

In what may be called the traditional hotel sector, individual properties are sometimes able to develop a market niche that is reflective of that particular hotel from a particular characteristic, such as location, physical structure or another individual characteristic. In the more concentrated industry sectors, such as the first class and luxury sectors, there are several hotel groups each with a large number of hotels. These groups are dependent on the service quality delivery rather than aspects of an individual property (Tepeci, 1999).

Thus it is particularly important to have a clear understanding of the expectations of consumers in relation to these hotel sectors because the higher levels of concentration and competition may increase guest complains. This research will address a number of literature gaps that exist in relation to the Indian and global hotel industries and will assist hotel managers, through a better understanding of the interrelationships between service quality, and customer satisfaction and to improve hotel performance and therefore customer satisfaction.

CHAPTER 1.1 (B)
TOURISM INDUSTRY – AN OVERVIEW

TOURISM INDUSTRY – GLOBAL PERSPECTIVE

Travel & Tourism is set for a milestone year as the industry's direct contribution to the global economy is expected to pass $2 trillion in GDP and 100 million jobs.

According to research by the World Travel & Tourism Council (WTTC), the global Travel & Tourism industry will grow by 2.8% in 2012, marginally faster than the global rate of economic growth, predicted to be 2.5%.

This rate of growth means that Travel & Tourism industry is expected to directly contribute $2 trillion to the global economy and sustain some 100.3 million jobs. When the wider economic impacts of the industry are taken into account, Travel & Tourism is forecast to contribute some $6.5 trillion to the global economy and generate 260 million jobs – or 1 in 12 of all jobs on the planet.

In 2011, Travel & Tourism's total economic contribution, taking account of its direct, indirect and induced impacts, was US$6.3 trillion in GDP, 255 million jobs, US$743 billion in investment and US$1.2 trillion in exports. This contribution represented 9% of GDP, 1 in 12 jobs, 5% of investment and 5% of exports.

David Scowsill, President & CEO of WTTC, said: "In 2012, when international travelers are expected to surpass one billion for the first time, the industry will pass two other major milestones: a direct contribution of $2 trillion to the world economy and 100 million jobs. But these numbers are dwarfed by the total forecast contribution of our industry – $6.5 trillion to the global economy and 260 million jobs."

Over the medium-term, the prospects of the industry are even more positive with average annual growth expected to be 4% through to 2022 by which time Travel & Tourism will employ 328 million people – or 1 in 10 of all jobs on the planet.

David Scowsill continued: "It is clear that the Travel & Tourism industry is going to be a significant driver of global growth and employment for the next decade. Our industry is responsible for creating jobs, pulling people out of poverty, and broadening horizons. It is one of the world's great industries".

Other selected highlights from the research show:

- South & Northeast Asia will be the fastest-growing regions in 2012, growing by 6.7%, driven by countries such as India and China where rising incomes will generate an increase in domestic tourism spend and a sharp upturn in capital investment, and recovery in Japan

- After an extremely challenging 2011 when civil unrest and violence had a dramatic impact on demand for Egypt, Tunisia and Libya, North Africa is showing signs of recovery in 2012 with Travel & Tourism direct GDP growth forecast at 3.6%. Morocco (8.3%) will be the star performer of this region as negative perceptions of security continue to affect tourism in Egypt and Tunisia

- In the Middle East, where civil unrest and violence in some countries continues, growth will be more subdued (3%), although there are stark differences at country level. Qatar will grow fastest at 13.2% while Syria will likely see another dramatic fall, estimated at 20.5%, as the political situation worsens, increasing concerns over security. It is worth noting that 14% of all international arrivals in the Middle East in 2010 were for Syria, the second most important destination in the region after Saudi Arabia

- The mature economies of North America and Europe will continue to struggle in 2012. North America, which is saw a slight upturn in the USA's economic situation at the end of 2011, should see growth of only 1.3% in Travel & Tourism direct GDP over the year

- The prospects for Travel & Tourism growth in Europe in 2012 are precarious. Current forecasts suggest a 0.3% increase in Travel & Tourism direct GDP for the region overall, but this will be propped up by newer economies such as Poland and, of course, Russia. A decline of 0.3% is expected across the European Union. Consumer spending is set to tighten as austerity measures kick in, and there continues to be considerable uncertainty around the future of the Eurozone and peripheral economies of Greece, Spain, Italy and Portugal.

In 2011 Travel & Tourism accounted for 255 million jobs globally. At US$6.3 trillion (9.1% of GDP) the sector is a key driver for investment and economic growth. For more than 20 years, the World Travel & Tourism Council has been the voice of this industry globally. Members are the Chairs, Presidents and Chief Executives of the world's leading, private sector Travel & Tourism businesses. These Members bring specialist knowledge to guide government policy and decision-making, raising awareness of the importance of the industry as an economic generator of prosperity.

Source: Research by the World Travel & Tourism Council (WTTC)

Key trends in 2011- 2012
• Demand for international tourism maintained momentum in 2011. International tourist arrivals grew by 4.6% to reach 983 million worldwide, up from 940 million in 2010.
• Europe, which accounts for over half of all international tourist arrivals worldwide, was the fastest-growing region, both in relative terms (+6% tied with Asia and the Pacific) and absolute terms (29 million more visitors).
• The Middle East (-8%) and North Africa (-9%) were the only (sub) regions to record a decline in arrivals, due to the Arab Spring and political transitions in the region.
• International tourism receipts for 2011 are estimated at US$ 1,030 billion worldwide, up from US$ 928 million in 2010 (+3.9% in real terms), setting new records in most destinations despite economic challenges in many source markets.

Current developments and outlook
• According to monthly and quarterly data for 2012 included in the *UNWTO World Tourism Barometer,* international tourist arrivals worldwide grew at a rate of 5% in the first four months of 2012, consolidating the growth trend that started in 2010.
• Forecasts prepared by UNWTO in January 2012 point to growth of 3% to 4% in international tourist arrivals for the full year 2012.
• Total international arrivals are expected to reach one billion in 2012 for the first time.

Long-term trends

• Over the past six decades, tourism has experienced continued expansion and diversification, becoming one of the largest and fastest-growing economic sectors in the world. Many new destinations have emerged, challenging the traditional ones of Europe and North America.

• Despite occasional shocks, international tourist arrivals have shown virtually uninterrupted growth – from 277 million in 1980 to 528 million in 1995, and 983 million in 2011.

• According to *Tourism Towards 2030*, UNWTO's recently updated, long-term outlook and assessment of future tourism trends, the number of international tourist arrivals worldwide is expected to increase by 3.3% a year on average from 2010 to 2030. This represents some 43 million more international tourist arrivals every year, reaching a total of 1.8 billion arrivals by 2030.

• In the past, emerging economy destinations have grown faster than advanced economy destinations, and this trend is set to continue in the future. Between 2010 and 2030, arrivals to emerging economies are expected to increase at double the pace (+4.4% a year) of those to advanced economies (+2.2% a year).

• As a result, the market share of emerging economies has increased from 30% in 1980 to 47% in 2011, and is expected to reach 57% by 2030, equivalent to over one billion international tourist arrivals.

INTERNATIONAL TOURISM

Key to development, prosperity and well-being

Over time, an ever increasing number of destinations have opened up and invested in tourism development, turning modern tourism into a key driver of socio-economic progress through export revenues, the creation of jobs and enterprises, and infrastructure development. As an internationally traded service, inbound tourism has become one of the world's major trade categories. The overall export income generated by inbound tourism, including passenger transport, exceeded US$ 1.2 trillion in 2011, or US$ 3.4 billion a day on average. Tourism exports account for as much as 30% of the world's exports of commercial services and 6% of overall exports of goods and services. Globally, as an export category, tourism ranks fourth after fuels, chemicals and food. For many developing countries it is one of the main sources of foreign exchange income and the number one export category, creating much needed employment and opportunities for development. The most comprehensive way to measure the economic importance of both inbound and domestic tourism in national economies is through the *2008 Tourism Satellite Account (TSA)*

Recommended Methodological Framework, approved by the UN Statistics Commission. Though many countries have taken steps towards the implementation of a TSA, relatively few have full, comparable results available. The knowledge and experience gained through the TSA exercise has certainly contributed to a much better understanding of the role of tourism in economies worldwide and allows for a tentative approximation of key indicators.

Based on the information from countries with data available, tourism's contribution to worldwide gross domestic product (GDP) is estimated at some 5%. Tourism's contribution to employment tends to be slightly higher and is estimated in the order of 6-7% of the overall number of jobs worldwide (direct and indirect). For advanced, diversified economies, the contribution of tourism to GDP ranges from approximately 2% for countries where tourism is a comparatively small sector, to over 10% for countries where tourism is an important pillar of the economy. For small islands and developing countries, the weight of tourism can be even larger, accounting for up to 25% in some destinations.

INTERNATIONAL TOURIST ARRIVALS

2011: Consolidation of growth despite multiple challenges

In 2011, world tourism continued to rebound from the setbacks of 2008-2009, in a year marked by persistent economic turbulence, major political changes in the Middle East and North Africa, and the natural disaster in Japan. Worldwide, international tourist arrivals (i.e. overnight visitors) grew by 4.6% in 2011 to 983 million, up from 940 million in 2010 when arrivals increased by 6.4%.

The majority of destinations around the world that had not exceeded pre-crisis levels in 2010 did so in 2011. Contrary to the long-term trend, advanced economies (+4.9%) posted higher growth than emerging economies (+4.3%), due largely to the strong results in Europe, and the setbacks in the Middle East and North Africa. Europe and Asia and the Pacific (both +6%) were the fastest-growing regions in terms of tourist arrivals in 2011. Europe grew above expectations, despite continuing economic uncertainty, while arrivals in Asia and the Pacific increased at a slower pace over 2010, partly due to the temporary decline in the Japanese outbound market. Arrivals in the Americas (+4%) were boosted by South America (+9%), which continued to lead growth in the region for the second consecutive year. Popular uprisings in a number of countries in Africa and the Middle East during 2011 took a toll on tourism in both regions. Africa (+1%) recorded only a slight increase, due to the loss of visitors in North Africa, while the Middle East saw an 8% decline in arrivals.

WORLD TOURISM TRAFFIC

International tourism recovered strongly in 2010 from the blow it suffered due to the global financial crisis and economic recession. International tourist arrivals worldwide registered a positive growth of 6.6% during the year 2010 as compared to negative growth of 3.8% during 2009 over 2008. The international tourist arrivals during 2010, 2009 and 2008 were 940 million, 882 million and 917 million respectively. France maintained the top position in terms of arrivals in 2010, followed by USA, China, Spain, Italy, UK, Turkey, Germany, Malaysia and Mexico. These top 10 countries accounted for 44.42% share of international tourist arrivals in 2010. As regards the regions, the highest tourist arrivals were in Europe, which attracted 476.6 million tourists in 2010, with a positive growth of 3.3% over 2009, followed by Asia & the Pacific with 203.8 million tourists with 12.7% growth over 2009, Americas with 149.8 million tourists with growth of 6.4% over 2009, Middle East with 60.3 million tourists with growth of 14.1% over 2009 and Africa with 49.4 million tourists with growth of 7.3% over 2009. In fact, in all these regions, positive growth was registered during the year 2010 over 2009. Table1.(B).1 gives the summary of international tourist arrivals in different regions of the world from 2008 to 2010.

INTERNATIONAL TOURISM RECEIPTS

As per UNWTO estimates, worldwide receipts from international tourism were US$ 919 billion in 2010, up from US$ 851 billion in 2009. All regions posted positive growth with the exception of Europe (-1.1%). Asia and the Pacific (22.4%) and Middle East (19.8%) showed the highest growth, while Africa (9.7%) and Americas (9.6%) posted comparatively better growth than world average.

TABLE 1(B).1

INTERNATIONAL TOURIST ARRIVALS WORLDWIDE AND BY REGIONS DURING 2009-2011

(Arrivals in millions)

Region	2009	2010	2011
World			
Arrivals	882.0	940.0	983.0
% Annual Change	-3.8	6.6	6.4
Africa			
Arrivals	46.0	49.4	50.2
% Annual Change	3.7	7.3	8.5
% Share in world	5.2	5.2	5.1

Region	2009	2010	2011
America			
Arrivals	140.6	149.8	156.6
% Annual Change	-4.9	6.4	6.4
% Share in world	15.9	15.9	15.9
Asia & the Pacific			
Arrivals	180.9	203.8	217
% Annual Change	-1.7	12.7	12.9
% Share in world	20.5	21.7	22.1
Europe			
Arrivals	461.5	476.6	504
% Annual Change	-4.9	3.3	2.8
% Share in world	52.3	50.7	51.3
Middle east			
Arrivals	52.9	60.3	55.4
% Annual Change	-4.3	14.1	14.2
% Share in world	6.0	6.4	5.6
India			
Arrivals	5.17	5.78	6.1
% Annual Change	-2.2	11.8	11.8
% Share in world	0.59	0.61	0.64

Source: United Nations World Tourism Organization (UNWTO)

INDIA TOURISM RECEIPTS - 2011

Table1. (B).1 gives the year-wise receipts from international tourism by regions during the years 2009-2011. During the year 2011, Europe accounted for about 44.2% of the world's total receipts from international tourism followed by Asia & the Pacific region (27.1%),

Americas (19.8%), Middle East (5.5%) and Africa (3.4%)

INTERNATIONAL TOURISM RECEIPTS WORLDWIDE AND BY REGIONS

The international tourism receipts worldwide and India's share in them during the years 1997-2011 are given in Table1.(B).2 The share of India in the world tourism receipts has remained between 0.65% and 0.72% during 1997-2002. However, it has been increasing steadily since 2002, and has reached 24.6% during 2010 - 2012

TABLE 1(B).2
INTERNATIONAL TOURISM RECEIPTS WORLDWIDE AND BY REGIONS, 2008-2010

(Receipts in Billion US$)

Region	2009	2010	2011
World			
Receipts	939.0	851.0	919.0
% Annual Change	9.6	-9.4	8.0
Africa			
Receipts	30.3	28.8	31.6
% Annual Change	4.5	-4.9	9.7
% Share in world	3.2	3.4	3.4
America			
Receipts	189.0	166.2	182.2
% Annual Change	10.3	-12.1	1 9.6
% Share in world	20.1	19.4	19.8

Region	2009	2010	2011
Asia and the Pacific			
Receipts	208.5	203.1	248.7
% Annual Change	11.5	-2.6	22.4
% Share in world	22.2	23.8	27.1
Region			
Europe			
Receipts	471.7	410.9	406.2
% Annual Change	8.4	-12.9	-1.1
% Share in world	50.2	48.5	44.2
Middle east			
Receipts	39.9	42.0	50.3
% Annual Change	15.3	5.3	19.8
% Share in world	4.2	4.9	5.5
Region	2009	2010	2011
India			
Receipts	11.83	11.39	17.19
% Annual Change	10.3	-3.7	24.6
% Share in world	10.3	-3.7	24.6

Source: UNWTO Tourism Highlights 2012 Edition

TOURISM IN INDIA

India boasts of the world's highest mountains, miles of coastline with excellent beaches, tropical forests and wildlife, adventure tourism, desert safari, lagoon backwaters, ancient monuments and World Heritage Sites, forts and palaces, and of course, the Taj Mahal. The Indian tourism and hospitality industry has thus emerged as one of the key sectors driving the country's growth. The tourism sector is thriving, owing to a huge surge in both business and leisure travel by foreign and domestic tourists.

According to the latest Tourism Satellite Accounting (TSA) research, released by the World Travel and Tourism Council (WTTC) and its strategic partner Accenture, India's travel and tourism industry is expected to generate almost US$ 275.5 billion by 2018, growing at an average of 9.4 per cent over the next ten years. Moreover, according to the TSA research, travel and tourism is expected to contribute 6.1 per cent to India's national gross domestic product (GDP) and provide almost 40 million jobs by 2018. Also, a country brand index (CBI) 2008 survey, conducted by Future Brand—a leading global brand consultancy—in collaboration with public relations firm Weber Shandwick's Global Travel & Lifestyle Practice, has ranked India second in the value-for-money index.

The rapid growth of India's tourism industry has been instrumental in South Asia being the preferred tourist destination as noted by the UN World Tourism Organization (UNWTO). Foreign tourist arrivals during the period January–October 2008 increased by 370,000 to 4.32 million as compared to 3.95 million during the corresponding period of 2007. Number of foreigners visiting India as tourists in October 2008 was 453,000 as compared to 331,000 in September 2008. Consequently, foreign exchange earnings from tourism in India rose from US$ 8.293 billion during January to October 2007 to US$ 9.696 billion during January to October 2008. Earlier, in 2007, total number of foreign tourists visiting India was 5.08 million - an increase of 14.3 per cent over 2006.

It is important that the industry focuses on social and environmental as well as economic benefits of tourism. This is not to suggest that economic considerations are mutually exclusive from those of social cohesion and the environment. In fact, sustainable economic returns can only be achieved through factoring in strategies that take all three elements into account.

The emphasis on tourism will increase due to:

- The continuing economic shift from traditional to service based industries;
- Greater focus caused by terrorism and airline crises in 2001 that highlighted the depth of tourism influence on economies and communities;
- Concentration on industries with capacity to increase export earnings; and
- Tourism being one of the few established industry sectors projected to maintain significant growth over a long period.

ECONOMIC IMPACT OF TOURISM IN INDIA

Tourism is one of India's largest industries. It accounts for $48.7 billion or 8.6% of India's Gross Domestic Product. This represents a greater contribution than the agriculture or communication services sectors. For India, tourism is worth $8.5 billion to the State's economy, contributing 5.2% to India's Gross State Product.

As part of the international economy, tourism is a major force as it generates 11.2% of India's total export earnings, more than traditional exports such as coal, iron and steel products. It is forecast that tourism's export growth rate will outperform all key sectors by 2004-2005. Tourism is an important economic driver. In India, $11 billion was spent by domestic and international visitors in 1998.

Revised forecasts from the Tourism Forecasting Council predict international visitor arrivals to India reached 9.4 million by the year 2010. International visitors are forecast to grow at an average annual rate of 6.6% over the next 10 years.

The Indian economy is fundamentally shifting from primary industry to a service and knowledge base. The total number of jobs increased by 17.3% between 1986 and 1996, but employment in agriculture (11%) and mining (6%) declined. Farming is losing its position as the primary industry of most rural economies. Decreasing farm profitability and labour efficiencies from agricultural technology and mechanization have changed rural employment.

Tourism can promote and facilitate economic activity that supports aspects of regional life. For example, farm stays, cellar doors and the purchase of local produce support agriculture, while the purchase of other products supports local retail and industry. Tourism spending also has a multiplier effect in the local economy as it is spent and re-spent by employers and employees.

Tourism may generate income for local government in the form of rates and levies or as a result of patronage of local government owned attractions and services. This income contributes to the quality and quantity of local services and facilities provided for the benefit of both residents and visitors.

Tourism in India is the largest service industry, with a contribution of 6.23% to the national GDP and 8.78% of the total employment in India. India witness's more than 17.9 million annual foreign tourist arrivals and 740 million domestic tourism visits. The tourism industry in India generated about US$100 billion in 2008 and that is expected to increase to US$275.5 billion by 2018 at a 9.4% annual growth rate. In the year 2010, 17.9 million foreign tourists visited India. Majority of foreign tourists come from USA and UK. Maharashtra, Tamil Nadu, Delhi, Uttar Pradesh and Rajasthan are the top 5 states to receive inbound tourists. Domestic tourism in the same year was massive at

740 million. Andhra Pradesh, Uttar Pradesh, Tamil Nadu and Maharashtra received the big share of these visitors. Ministry of Tourism is the nodal agency to formulate national policies and programmes for the development and promotion of tourism. In the process, the Ministry consults and collaborates with other stakeholders in the sector including various Central Ministries/agencies, the State Governments/ union Territories and the representatives of the private sector. Concerted efforts are being made to promote new forms of tourism such as rural, cruise, medical and eco-tourism. The Ministry of Tourism is the nodal agency for the development and promotion of tourism in India and maintains the Incredible India campaign.

According to *World Travel and Tourism Council*, India will be a tourism hotspot from 2009–2018, having the highest 10-year growth potential. The *Travel & Tourism Competitiveness Report 2007* ranked tourism in India 6th in terms of price competitiveness and 39th in terms of safety and security. Despite short- and medium-term setbacks, such as shortage of hotel rooms, tourism revenues are expected to surge by 42% from 2007 to 2017. India's 5,000 years of history, its length, breadth and the variety of geographic features make its tourism basket large and varied. It presents heritage and cultural tourism along with medical, business and sports tourism. India has a growing medical tourism sector..

Source- Wikipedia

IMPORTANT HIGHLIGHT OF INDIAN TOURISM INDUSTRY
• The number of Foreign Tourist Arrivals (FTAs) in India during 2011 increased to 6.29 million as compared to 5.17 million in 2009. The growth rate in FTAs during 2011 over 2009 was 8.9% as compared to (-) 2.2% during 2009 over 2008. The growth rate of 11.8% in 2010 for India was better than UNWTO's projected growth rate of 5% to 6% for the world in 2010.
• The share of India in international tourist arrivals in 2011 was 0.61%, which is 0.02% improvement over 2009. However, India's rank improved to 40th, in 2010, from 41st in

2009. India accounted for 2.83% of tourist arrivals in Asia Pacific Region in 2010, with the rank of 11.

• About 91.8% of the FTAs entered India through air routes followed by 7.5% by land routes and 0.7% by sea routes. Delhi and Mumbai airports accounted for about 54.9% of the total FTAs in India. The top 15 source markets for FTAs in India in 2010 were USA, UK, Bangladesh, Sri Lanka, Canada, Germany, France, Malaysia, Australia, Japan, Russian Fed., China(Main), Singapore, Nepal and Republic of Korea. These 15 countries accounted for about 71.86% of total FTAs in India in 2010.

• Tourism continues to play an important role as a foreign exchange earner for the country. In 2010, foreign exchange earnings (FEE) from tourism were US$ 14.19 billion as compared to US$ 11.39 billion in 2009, registering a growth of 24.6%.

• Number of domestic tourist visits in India during 2010 was 740.21 million as compared to 668.80 million in 2009, with a growth rate of 18.8 %.

• Number of Indian national departures from India during 2010 was 12.99 million as compared to 11.07 million in 2009, registering a growth rate of 17.4%.

Table 1(B).3
Foreign Tourist Arrivals (FTAs) and Foreign Exchange Earnings (FEE) from Tourism in India during 2011 and comparative figures of 2010 and 2009

Foreign Tourist Arrivals (FTAs) and Foreign Exchange Earnings (FEE) from Tourism in India during 2011 and comparative figures of 2010 and 2009					
Foreign Tourist Arrivals (Nos)					
Month		Foreign Tourist Arrivals (Nos.)		Percentage Change	
2009	2010 (R)	2011 @	2010/09	2011/10	
January	481308	568719	623885	18.2%	9.7%
February	489787	552152	635527	12.7%	15.1%
March	442062	512152	550051	15.9%	7.4%
April	347544	371956	437792	7.0%	17.7%
May	305183	332087	355333	8.8%	7.0%

June	352353	384642	412336	9.2%	7.2%
July	432900	466715	513853	7.8%	10.1%
August	369707	422173	444548	14.2%	5.3%
September	330707	369821	401995	11.8%	8.7%
October	458849	507093	562873	10.5%	11.0%
November	541524	608178	636762	12.3%	4.7%
December	615775	680004	715364	10.4%	5.2%
Total	5167699	5775692	6290319	11.8%	8.9%

Foreign Exchange Earnings (in Rs. Crore)

Month		Foreign Exchange Earnings (in Rs. Crore)		Percentage Change	
2009 #	2010 #	2011 #	2010/09	2011/10	
January	4598	5593	5777	21.6%	3.3%
February	4547	6646	7653	46.2%	15.2%
March	4437	5507	5522	24.1%	0.3%
April	4061	4518	5724	11.3%	26.7%
May	3249	4358	5047	34.1%	15.8%
June	3801	4751	5440	25.0%	14.5%
July	4983	5444	7116	9.3%	30.7%
August	4115	4620	5734	12.3%	24.1%
September	3798	4678	5748	23.2%	22.9%
October	4806	5219	7019	8.6%	34.5%
November	5523	6516	7941	18.0%	21.9%
December	7042	7039	8870	0.0%	26.0%
Total	54960	64889	77591	18.1%	19.6%

Foreign Exchange Earnings(in US$ million)

Month		Foreign Exchange Earnings (in US$ million)		Percentage Change	
2009 #	2010 #	2011 #	2010/09	2011/10	
January	941	1215	1273	29.1%	4.8%

February	923	1434	1684	55.4%	17.4%
March	867	1209	1227	39.4%	1.5%
April	811	1013	1290	24.9%	27.3%
May	669	951	1124	42.2%	18.2%
June	796	1020	1213	28.1%	18.9%
July	1028	1163	1603	13.1%	37.8%
August	851	992	1264	16.6%	27.4%
September	785	1015	1208	29.3%	19.0%
October	1028	1175	1424	14.3%	21.2%
November	1185	1448	1566	22.2%	8.1%
December	1510	1558	1688	3.2%	8.3%
Total	11394	14193	16564	24.6%	16.7%

@ Provisional Estimates # Advance Estimates R: Revised

Source: Tourism survey 2011 www.tourism.gov.in

INDIAN TOURISM STATISTICS 2011 - 2012

INDIA REGISTERED 6.81 LAKH VISITORS IN JANUARY 2012

Foreign Tourist Arrivals (FTAs) during January, 2012 numbered 6.81 lakh as compared to FTAs of 6.24 lakh during January, 2011 and 5.69 lakh in January, 2010. The trend of positive growth in FTAs observed during 2011 continued in January, 2012 too with a growth rate of 9.2 per cent. The growth rate of 9.2 per cent in January 2012 over January 2011 was higher than the 5.2 per cent growth rate observed in December, 2011 over December 2010.

Foreign Exchange Earnings (FEE) during January 2012 were Rs 8,623 crore as compared to Rs 5,777 crore in January 2011 and Rs 5,593 crore in January 2010. The growth rate in FEE in rupee terms in January 2012 over January 2011 was 49.3 per cent as compared to 3.3 per cent in January 2011 over January 2010. FEE in USD terms during January 2012 were USD 1,681 million as compared to FEE of USD 1,273 million during January 2011 and USD 1,215 million in January 2010. The growth rate in FEE in USD terms in January 2012 over January 2011 was 32.1 per cent as compared to the growth of 4.8 per cent in January 2011 over January 2010.

INDIA RECEIVES 6.77 LAKH FOREIGNERS IN FEBRUARY 2012

Continuing the growth trend, India received 6.77 lakh foreign tourists in February 2012 as against 6.36 lakh visitors in the corresponding period last year, an increase of 6.6 per cent, according to a PTI report. The foreign exchange earnings from tourism also increased to Rs 8,502 crore in February 2012 as compared to Rs 7,653 crore in February 2011, a growth of 11.1 percent.

The World Travel and Tourism Council have ranked India as a tourism hot-spot with a very high growth possibility in the coming years. "The Ministry of Tourism has set a target of attracting 11 million foreign tourists by 2016. We have undertaken a series of road shows abroad and as per our plan we will be showcasing our destinations in more countries in coming years to reach the target," a senior Ministry of Tourism official said.

Source: By HBI Staff | Mumbai

India records 4.52 lakh foreign tourist arrivals in April 2012

India recorded 4.52 lakh foreign tourist arrivals (FTAs) during April, 2012, a 3.3 per cent growth as compared to FTAs of 4.38 lakh during the month of April, 2011 and 3.72 lakh in April, 2010, informed a PIB release. The lower growth this year is partly due to the high base growth rate in April 2011 over April 2010. FTAs during the period January-April 2012 were 24.34 lakh with a growth of 8.3 per cent as compared to FTAs of 22.47 lakh with a growth of 12.1 per cent during January-April 2011 over the corresponding period of 2010.

Foreign exchange earnings (FEE) during April 2012 were Rs 6,745 crore as compared to Rs 5,724 crore in April 2011 and Rs 4,518 crore in April 2010. The growth rate in FEE in rupee terms in April 2012 over April 2011 was 17.8 per cent as compared to 26.7 per cent in April 2011 over April 2010. FEE in USD terms during April 2012 were USD 1,305 million as compared to FEE of USD 1,290 million during the month of April 2011 and USD 1,013 million in April 2010. The growth rate in FEE in USD terms in April 2012 over April 2011 was 1.2 per cent as compared to a growth of 27.3 per cent in April 2011 over April 2010. FEE from tourism in terms of USD during January-April 2012 was USD 6,274 million with a growth of 14.6 per cent as compared to USD 5,474 million with a growth of 12.4 per cent during January-April, over the corresponding period of 2010.

Source: Wednesday, May 09, 2012, 13:00 Hrs [IST]

By HBI Staff | Mumbai

India receives 4.15 lakh FTAs in Sept 2012

India recorded 4.15 lakh Foreign Tourist Arrivals (FTAs) in September, 2012 as compared to FTAs of 4.02 lakh during the same period last year, registering a growth of 3.2 per cent. From January to September 2012, 46.33 lakh foreign tourists visited India as compared to 43.75 lakh FTAs during the corresponding period last year, which is a growth of 9.9 per cent.

The country's Foreign Exchange Earnings (FEE) during September 2012 were Rs 6652 crore as compared to Rs 5748 crore last September. The growth rate in FEE in rupee terms in September 2012 over September 2011 was 15.7 per cent as compared to 22.9

per cent in September 2011. FEEs from tourism in rupee terms during January-September 2012 were Rs 66061 crore with a growth of 22.9 per cent, as compared to the FEEs of Rs 53761 crore during January- September 2011 over the corresponding period of 2010.

FEEs in USD terms during September, 2012 were USD 1219 million as compared to FEEs of USD 1208 million of last September. The growth rate in FEEs in USD terms in September 2012 over September 2011 was 0.9 per cent. FEEs from tourism in terms of USD during January to September 2012 were USD 12492 million with a growth of 5.1 per cent, as compared to USD 11886 million with a growth of 18.7 per cent during January- September 2011 over the corresponding period of 2010.

Source: Friday, October 12, 2012, 14:00 Hrs [IST]

By HBI Staff | Mumbai

FOREIGN TOURIST ARRIVALS

TABLE 1(B).4:

NATIONALITY-WISE FOREIGN TOURIST ARRIVALS IN INDIA, 2008-2010

NATIONALITY-WISE FOREIGN TOURIST ARRIVALS IN INDIA, 2008-2010								
Country of Nationality		**Number of Arrivals**		**% Share**			**% Change**	
2008	**2009**	**2010**	**2008**	**2009**	**2010**	**2009/08**	**2010/09**
North America								
Canada	222364	224069	242372	4.21	4.34	4.20	0.8	8.2
U.S.A	804933	827140	931292	15.24	16.01	16.12	2.8	12.6
Total	1027297	1051209	1173664	19.45	20.34	20.32	2.3	11.6
Central and South America								
Argentina	5087	6011	7626	0.10	0.12	0.13	18.2	26.9
Brazil	11530	13964	15219	0.22	0.27	0.26	21.1	9.0
Mexico	9272	8185	10458	0.18	0.16	0.18	-11.7	27.8
Others	17616	18444	29425	0.33	0.36	0.51	4.7	59.5

Total	43505	46604	62728	0.82	0.90	1.09	7.1	34.6
Western Europe								
Austria	25900	27930	32620	0.49	0.54	0.56	7.8	16.8
Belgium	36277	34759	37709	0.69	0.67	0.65	-4.2	8.5
Denmark	34253	30857	35541	0.65	0.60	0.62	-9.9	15.2
Finland	29223	24874	24089	0.55	0.48	0.42	-14.9	-3.2
France	207802	196462	225232	3.93	3.80	3.90	-5.5	14.6
Germany	204344	191616	227720	3.87	3.71	3.94	-6.2	18.8
Greece	6672	6664	7441	0.13	0.13	0.13	-0.1	11.7
Ireland	18924	19223	20329	0.36	0.37	0.35	1.6	5.8
Italy	85766	77873	94100	1.62	1.51	1.63	-9.2	20.8
Netherlands	71605	64580	70756	1.36	1.25	1.23	-9.8	9.6
Norway	22369	22092	22229	0.42	0.43	0.38	-1.2	0.6
Portugal	15415	17184	21038	0.29	0.33	0.36	11.5	22.4
Spain	62535	59047	72591	1.18	1.14	1.26	-5.6	22.9
Sweden	58961	43327	45028	1.12	0.84	0.78	-26.5	3.9
Switzerland	42107	38290	43134	0.80	0.74	0.75	-9.1	12.7
U.K.	776530	769251	759494	14.70	14.89	13.15	-0.9	-1.3
Others	10842	10013	11291	0.21	0.19	0.20	-7.6	12.8
Total	1709525	1634042	1750342	32.36	31.62	30.31	-4.4	7.1
Eastern Europe								
Czech Rep.	8549	8328	9918	0.16	0.16	0.17	-2.6	19.1
Hungary	5263	4980	6022	0.10	0.10	0.10	-5.4	20.9
Kazakhstan	7534	6848	8786	0.14	0.13	0.15	-9.1	28.3
Poland	23517	19656	25424	0.45	0.38	0.44	-16.4	29.3
Russia	91095	94945	122048	1.72	1.84	2.11	4.2	28.5
Ukraine	12344	12436	16462	0.23	0.24	0.29	0.7	32.4
Others	42808	36282	38990	0.81	0.70	0.68	-15.2	7.5
Total	191110	183475	227650	3.62	3.55	3.94	-4.0	24.1
Africa								

Egypt	5326	5869	8017	0.10	0.11	0.14	10.2	36.6
Kenya	14941	22704	29223	0.28	0.44	0.51	52.0	28.7
Mauritius	19713	18866	21672	0.37	0.37	0.38	-4.3	14.9
Nigeria	13997	18338	23893	0.26	0.35	0.41	31.0	30.3
South Africa	42337	44308	55688	0.80	0.86	0.96	4.7	25.7
Sudan	3473	4987	7418	0.07	0.10	0.13	43.6	48.7
Tanzania	14872	17020	17645	0.28	0.33	0.31	14.4	3.7
Others	27091	32382	40969	0.51	0.63	0.71	19.5	26.5
Total	141750	164474	204525	2.68	3.18	3.54	16.0	24.4
West Asia								
Bahrain	7224	7901	7766	0.14	0.15	0.13	9.4	-1.7

TABLE 1(B).5:

IMPORTANT STATISTICS ON TOURISM, 2011- 2012

(I) INDIA

1. Number of Foreign Tourist Arrivals in India (million) 983(P)
Annual Growth Rate 4.6%

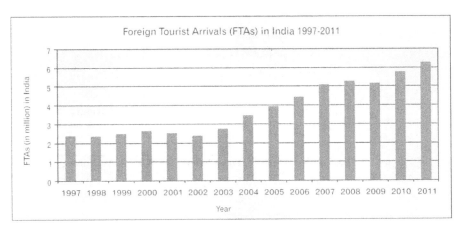

Source – Ministry of Tourism, Govt. of India, for 2011-2012

Fig: 1(B).1 Foreign Tourist Arrivals in India 1997- 2011

| **2. Number of Sea Cruise Passengers (million) 0.105** |
| Annual Growth Rate 17.3% |

| **3. Foreign Tourist Arrivals by Mode of Transport (Percentage)** |
| i) Air 91.8 |
| ii) Land 7.5 |
| iii) Sea 0.7 |

4. Foreign Tourist Arrivals by Port of Entry (Numbers in million and Percentage share)	
i) Delhi (Airport)	1.99(34.4%)
ii) Mumbai (Airport)	1.18(20.5%)
iii) Chennai (Airport)	0.62(10.7%)
iv) Bangalore (Airport)	0.37(6.5%)
v) Haridaspur (Land Check post)	0.24(4.2%)
vi) Kolkata (Airport)	0.21(3.7%)
vii) Dabolim-Goa (Airport)	0.17(3.0%)
viii) Hyderabad (Airport)	0.17(2.9%)
ix) Trivandrum (Airport)	0.12(2.0%)
x) Cochin (Airport)	0.11(1.9%)
xi) Others	0.60 (10.2%)
xii) All Ports	5.78(100.0%)

5. Foreign Tourist Arrivals From Top 10 Markets (Numbers in million and Percentage share)	
i) U.S.A.	1.004 (15.97%)
ii) UK	0.791(12.57%)
iii) Bangladesh	0.399 (6.34%)
iv) Sri Lanka	0.305(4.8%)

v) Canada	0.255(4.05%)
vi) Germany	0.253(4.02%)
vii) France	0.237 (3.76%)
viii) Malaysia	0.218 (3.46%)
ix) Japan	0.189 (3.01%)
x) Australia	0.186 (2.96%)
Total of top 10 countries	3.837 (60.98%)
Others	2.453 (39.02%)
All Countries	6.290 (100%)

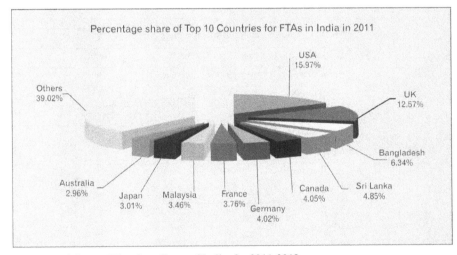

Source – Ministry of Tourism, Govt. of India, for 2011-2012

Fig: 1(B).2 Percentage share of top 10 countries for FTAs in India in 2011

6. Foreign Exchange Earnings from Tourism
i) In INR terms (1 crore = 10 million) Rs. 77591 crore
Annual Growth Rate 19.6%
ii) In US$ terms US$ 16.56 billion
Annual Growth Rate 16.7%

7. No. of Indian Nationals Departures from India (million) 12.99
Annual Growth Rate 17.4%

8. Number of Domestic Tourist Visits (million) 740.21(P)
Annual Growth Rate 10.7%

9. Approved Hotels as on 31st December 2010
i) Number of Hotels 2483
ii) Number of Rooms 117815

10. Travel Trade as on 31st December 2010	
i) Number of Approved Tour Operators	600
ii) Number of Approved Travel Agencies	467
iii) Number of Approved Tourist Transport Operators	213
iv) Number of Approved Domestic Tour Operators	67
v) Number of Approved Adventure Tour Operators	33

(II) WORLD

1. Number of International Tourist Arrivals (million)	940.0 (P)
Annual Growth Rate	6.6%
2. International Tourism Receipts	(US$ billion) 919.0(P)
Annual Growth Rate	8.0%

(III) ASIA PACIFIC REGION

1. Number of International Tourist Arrivals (million)	203.8 (P)
Annual Growth Rate	12.7%
2. International Tourism Receipts	(US$ billion) 248.7 (P)
Annual Growth Rate	22.4%

(IV) INDIA'S POSITION IN WORLD

1. Share of India in International Tourist Arrivals	0.61%
2. India's rank in World Tourist Arrivals	38
3. Share of India in International Tourism Receipts	1.61%
4. India's rank in World Tourism Receipts	17

(V) INDIA'S POSITION IN ASIA PACIFIC REGION

1. Share of India in Tourist Arrivals	2.90%
2. India's rank in Tourist Arrivals	9
3. Share of India in Tourism Receipts	5.72%
4. India's rank in Tourism Receipts	8

(P) Provisional # Advance Estimates

FOREIGN EXCHANGE EARNINGS FROM TOURISM IN INDIA

For the FEE's, tourism is the most important sector in the country. As per the monthly estimates prepared by Ministry of Tourism, FEE from tourism in India in 2010 was Rs` 64889 crore as compared to Rs 54960 in 2009 registering a growth of 18.1 % in 2010 over 2009. In US $ term, FEE from tourism in 2010 were US $ 14.19 billion as compared to US$ 11.39 billion in 2009 with a growth rate of 24.6%. FEE from tourism in 2010 were US $ 16.56 billion. In 2011 the FEE from tourism in India, in INR terms was 77591 and US$ terms was 16.56 billion. FEE from tourism in India, in INR terms and US$ terms during 2001-2012 are given in Table 2.10.1.

TABLE 1(B).6:

FOREIGN EXCHANGE EARNINGS FROM TOURISM IN INDIA DURING

2001-2012

Year	FEE in ` Rs terms		FEE in US$ terms	
	` Crore	% Change over previous year	US $ Million	% Change over previous year
2001	15083	-3.5	3198	-7.6
2002	15064	-0.1	3103	15064
2003	20729	37.6	4463	43.8
2004	27944	34.8	6170	38.2
2005	33123	18.5	7493	21.4
2006	39025	17.8	8634	15.2
2007	44360	13.7	10729	24.3
2008	51294	15.6	11832	10.3
2009	54960	7.1	11394	-3.7
2010	64889	18.1	14193	24.6
2011	77591	19.6	16564	16.7
2012 (Jan to June	43760	@24.4	8455	@8.2

TABLE 1(B).7

DOMESTIC AND FOREIGN TOURIST VISITS IN FIVE STATES/UT, 2009-

2011

State/UT	2009		2010		2011		% Growth (2010/11)	
	Domestic	Foreign	Domestic	Foreign	Domestic	Foreign	Domestic	Foreign
Delhi	8834047	1958272	13558353	1893650	1633456	2159925	53.5	-3.3
Karnataka	32701647	326944	38202077	380995	84107390	574005	16.8	16.5
Madhya Pradesh	23106206	200819	38079595	250430	44119820	23312	64.8	24.7

| Maharashtra | 30628394 | 2426362 | 48465492 | 5083126 | 55333467 | 4814421 | 58.2 | 109.5 |
| Rajasthan | 25558691 | 1073414 | 25543877 | 1278523 | 27137323 | 1351974 | -0.1 | 19.1 |

APPROVED HOTELS

The Ministry of Tourism has adopted a system of approving and classifying the hotels on the basis of the facilities and services provided by them.

The category-wise details regarding the number of hotels and hotel rooms available during the years 2009 and 2010 are presented below:

TABLE 1(B).8:

NUMBER OF APPROVED HOTELS AND AVAILABILITY OF HOTEL ROOMS

DURING 2009 AND 2010 IN KARNATAKA

tates/UTs	5 Star Deluxe	5 Star	4 Star	3 Star	2 Star	1 Star	Apartment hotel	Time share hotel	Heritage	Silver and gold B&B	Total
o. of Hotels	9	10	4	34	6	7	2	1	3	4	80
o. of Rooms	1480	1474	351	1946	332	384	250	62	121	8	6408

TABLE 1(B).9:

ANALYSIS OF HOTEL GUESTS, 2009-10 BY CATEGORY OF HOTELS

Composition	5 star deluxe	5 star	4 star	3 star	2 star	1 star	Heritage	Others	All India average
Number of Responses	41	42	80	397	215	47	34	59	915
Domestic Guests (%)	48.5	54.1	61.7	76.4	83.9	83.7	43.0	85.3	74.1
Foreign Guests (%)	51.5	45.9	38.3	23.6	16.1	16.3	57.0	14.7	25.9
Total	100.0	100.0	100.0	100.0	100.0	100.0	100.0	100.0	100.0

Total Business Guests(%)	63.9	61.0	64.4	62.3	60.3	61.0	25.0	58.0	60.4
Total Leisure Guests (%)	36.1	39.0	35.6	37.7	39.8	39.0	75.0	42.0	39.7
Total	**100.0**	**100.0**	**100.0**	**100.0**	**100.0**	**100.0**	**100.0**	**100.0**	**100.0**
Avg. Stay of Foreign Guests (Days)	3.1	4.4	4.0	3.4	3.1	2.9	2.9	2.5	3.3
Avg. tay of Domestic Guest (Days)	2.1	3.1	2.6	3.2	3.0	3.5	2.6	2.6	3.0
Avg. Stay of Business Guests (Days)	2.3	3.4	3.3	3.6	3.0	2.6	2.2	2.9	3.2
Avg. Stay of leisure Guests (Days)	2.2	2.9	2.4	2.7	2.6	3.4	2.1	3.0	2.6
Repeat Guests(%)	35.9	35.3	40.3	47.1	51.8	47.7	24.2	49.3	45.9

Source: India Tourism statistics 2010, www.tourism.gov.in, www.incredibleindia.org, Government of India, Ministry of Tourism, Market research Division

The Federation of Hotel & Restaurant Associations of India (FHRAI) collects information from its members through a questionnaire for its annual Indian Hotel Industry Survey, which is analysed and presented in a report. For the year 2009-10 (April-March), FHRAI received information from 1200 members.

Based on FHRAI's 2009-10 survey, information on various aspects of hotel industry in India like profile of an average hotel, average number of employees per hotel, average percentage of trained employees per hotel and Guest Analysis is presented in Tables below

Following are the important highlights of the data presented in these tables:–

• Most of the rooms in all categories of hotels were air-conditioned.

• Average employee per room for all categories of hotels taken together was 1.5. Among the classified categories, variation was quite low: 1.0 in 1-Star & 2-Star categories and 2.0 in 5-Star Deluxe categories.

• 78.1% of the employees were trained: highest being 86.3% under Heritage and lowest 72.8% under 1-Star category.

• Share of tourists is the highest from UK being 14.4%. Other countries and USA dominate the overall visitations with a share of 12.9% and 12.2% respectively.

• Share of tourists from UK and USA was the highest in the 2-Star and above category hotels.

• Share of tourists from UK & France was the highest in Heritage category hotels.

• Share of domestic guests was 74.1% for all the hotels taken together. However, share of foreign guests was higher in 5-Star Deluxe (51.5%) and Heritage (57.0%).

• Leisure tourists constituted about 39.7% of the total guests and the remaining 60.4% were business guests. Except the Heritage categories of hotels, share of business guests was higher in other categories.

• While the average stay of foreign guests was 3.3 days, it was 3.0 days for domestic guests.

• Average stay of business and leisure guests was 3.2 days and 2.6 days respectively.

TABLE 1(B).10:

AVERAGE PERCENTAGE OF TRAINED EMPLOYEES PER HOTEL, 2009-10
BY CATEGORY OF HOTELS

Composition	5 Star Deluxe	5 Star	4 Star	3 Star	2 Star	1 Star	Heritage	Others	All ave
Number of Responses	32	35	69	297	133	26	30	50	67.
No. of Managers	92.5	90.6	87.4	87.3	90.6	87.4	93.8	86.5	88.
No. of Supervisors	87.4	79.4	81.2	80.6	76.2	71.4	89.8	80.2	80.
No. of Staff	70.2	70.1	68.0	63.9	62.7	59.7	75.2	69.5	65.
Total Average Trained employees	83.3	80.0	78.9	77.3	76.5	72.8	86.3	78.7	78.
Total Average Un-Trained Employees	16.7	20.0	21.1	22.7	23.5	27.2	13.7	21.3	22.

Trained Employees includes those with a minimum one-year certificate course from a hotel management or equivalent institution, however, some hotels may have included those with short term (in-house) training.

Source: Indian Hotel Industry Survey 2009-2010, FHRAI

TOURISM INDUSTRY IN KARNATAKA

Karnataka is expecting to host more than five crore tourists in the coming years, including domestic and international, with an estimated 4.77 crore having already visited the southern State until July 2011.

According to Mr K. Viswanatha Reddy, Director of Tourism, Karnataka "In 2009, we received 3.29 crore tourists whose number swelled to 3.85 crore in 2010,"

While Karnataka Tourism has won many accolades and has been seen as India's best and the fourth most attractive destination in the world over, as per The Conde Nast Traveller, its inter-State packages have boosted the number recently.

In particular, the Rs 1,600 per head package for the Bangalore-Tirupati-Bangalore pilgrimage circuit has been received very well, he added.

This year (2011), over 5.5 lakh visitors have visited the official website, www.karnakatatourism.org so far. Among the domestic tourists, the maximum travel to Karnataka from Gujarat, Maharashtra and West Bengal.

According to the data provided by the Karnataka Tourism Department, the tourist arrivals in Karnataka between 2008 and 2010 were:

TABLE 1(B).12:

Tourist arrivals in Karnataka between 2008 and 2010

	Domestic	Foreign
2008	37,010,928	520,041
2009	32,729,679	229,847
2010	38,202,077	324,573

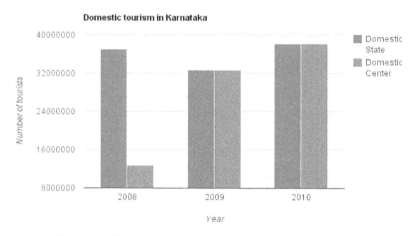

Fig: 1(B).3 Domestic tourism in Karnataka

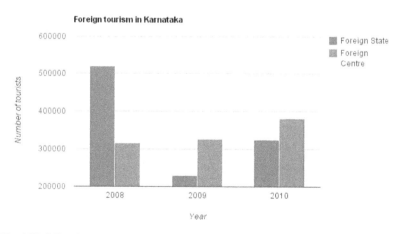

Fig: 1(B).4 Foreign tourism in Karnataka

Source: Bangalore (Dec. 8, 2011) - The statistics provided by the central and state
tourism departments regarding the number of tourist arrivals in Karnataka

HOSPITALITY INDUSTRY – BANGALORE

Prospects remain positive for Bangalore's hotel and tourism industries in the coming years, with more than 6,400 hotel rooms expected to be added in the next couple of years, including international hotel offerings from the Ritz-Carlton, Shangri-La and J.W Marriott.

In view of the substantial planned room additions, occupancies are forecasted to stabilize around 65-70 % in the next 5 years with daily room rate averaging at Rs.16,000.00

The tourism industry in Bangalore, which receives more business travelers than leisure tourists both from the international and domestic markets, is set for further growth by improvements made to the tourism infrastructure and the continued growth inbound arrivals.

Given its strategic location as a key gateway, particularly for domestic tourists, to the World Heritage sites and historical locations in the state, Bangalore is in a good position to further expand its leisure tourism potential.

Besides, the city is also aiming to become a healthcare hub by 2012, with heavy investments by the Manipal Group, Wockhardt and Columbia Asia to increase the number of hospital beds in the city.

Bangalore is leading the recovery in the domestic hotel industry. In the garden city, the rate of recovery was faster in the first half of the year compared to other business destinations like Mumbai and Delhi.

Bangalore witnessed a fall of as much as 47% in revenue per available room and around 5% drop in room demand in 2009-10. It has seen occupancy rates improving on a month-on-month basis, with February reporting the highest occupancy rate at 80% and average room rates touching close to the levels of early 2009 at Rs. 10,136.

In Mumbai, which took a double blow due to the recession and November 2008 terror attacks, the market is limping back gradually with average room rates during January-May 2010 at Rs. 9,071.8 as against Rs. 10,021.4 in the same period previous year, a fall of 9%. The occupancy rate for January-May 2010 stood at 67.5% as against 58.2% in the same period previous year.

"Post 26/11, the most severe fall in ARRs was witnessed in Bangalore, followed by Mumbai and Delhi. With occupancies now stabilising at close to 70%, we are witnessing a re-building of rates — which have started steadily climbing. The growth is highest in Bangalore (where the decline was the steepest). The process has also started in Mumbai and Delhi," says Rajiv Kaul, president, The Leela Palaces, Hotels and Resorts. The industry is expecting a growth of 8-10% in the third and fourth quarter across markets.

However, on a year-on-year basis, there is still a long way to go. According to the Crisil report, average room rates in Bangalore during the first five months of 2010 stood at around Rs. 8,843.6 as against Rs. 11,768.2 in the same period last year, a decline of 25%. On the other hand, occupancy rate has improved from 56.46% in January-May 2009 to 67.68% during January-May 2010.

Hotels in Bengaluru see rise in domestic traffic

The hospitality landscape is Bengaluru has always stood out in comparison to other cities like Mumbai and Delhi, both in pricing and customer profile. With the addition of over 3,000 rooms in the four and five-star categories in the last 18 months - most of them in micro markets away from the city centre, the international to domestic traffic ratio in hotels has become 50:50, from 80:20 four years ago.

As per a TOI report by Anshul Dhamija, there are two major reasons for this. Firstly, most of these micro markets such as Hosur Road, Sarjapur Road, Yeshwantpur and BEL Circle are located close to non-IT industry hubs, such as education, manufacturing, textile, and aerospace, which see a lot of domestic business traffic movement. Secondly, the addition of room inventory has resulted in competitive pricing, making hotel rooms more attractive to the price sensitive domestic traveler.

New entrants in the five-star category such as Movenpick Hotel & Spa, The Sheraton Bangalore Hotel at Brigade Gateway, Taj Vivanta in Yeshwantpur, and Novotel Bengaluru Techpark, have priced their rooms aggressively at Rs 6,500 to Rs 7,500 per night, with breakfast being complimentary, as per the report.

Biswajit Chakraborty, GM, The Movenpick Hotel & Spa, said, "The international to domestic traffic at Movenpick is 50:50." He added that the domestic traffic is on the rise even among IT companies.

Ajay Sampige, GM, Hotel ibis Bengaluru on Hosur Road, said Hosur has a mix of educational institutions, small and medium enterprises, and IT companies servicing Indian clients, and it creates a high volume of domestic traffic. "There is also a significant amount of leisure domestic traffic coming from people travelling from Chennai," he further said.

Chender Baljee, CMD, Royal Orchid Hotels, said that the number of new foreign companies setting up shop in Bengaluru has come down, impacting international business traffic volumes. "At the same time there has been a growth in domestic traffic, which is why the international to domestic traffic ratio at hotels have changed," he said, adding that the city's Average Room Rates (ARRs) are down by around 20-25 per cent compared to four years ago.

According to the report, domestic traffic accounts for 60 per cent of occupancy at ibis, which has rooms at Rs 4,499 per night, while at Novotel, the domestic traffic accounts for 40 per cent of occupancy. "It's encouraging to see the emergence of the domestic market as this market segment would shield the industry from any adverse headwinds coming from the US and Europe," said Puneet Dhawan, GM, ibis & Novotel Bengaluru Techpark.

Source: Wednesday, August 29, 2012, 11:00 Hrs [IST]

By HBI Staff | Mumbai

50,000 hotel rooms in top six Indian cities in 5 years: C&W – CII report

Cushman & Wakefield (C&W) jointly launched the research report with Confederation of Indian Industries (CII) titled 'Indian Hospitality Story 2012 & Beyond' at the fourth International CII Hospitality Fair 2012, which started yesterday in New Delhi, and will go on till September 22, 2012. The report was released by Subodh Kant Sahai, Minister for Tourism, Government of India.

In this report C&W evaluates the hospitality sector dynamics of top six cities of India - Bengaluru, Chennai, Delhi, Hyderabad, Kolkata and Mumbai and provides an overview on the performance, growth and outlook of the Indian hospitality industry.

According to the report, the top six cities of India are expected to see a total of 50,000 new hotel rooms across categories in the next five to six years. This is in response to the steady growth the hospitality sector has recorded over the last few years. 2012 alone is expected to see 14,800 fresh keys by the end of the year. Out of the total expected supply for 2012, 2000 new hotel rooms have already entered the market.

Akshay Kulkarni, Regional Director – Hospitality, South and South East Asia, Cushman & Wakefield, said "India's hospitality sector has been witnessing interest from a variety of segments ranging from - MICE, Wellness Tourism, Spiritual & Pilgrimage Tourism, apart from the traditional business or leisure travel. The demand has been strong from both foreign as well as domestic tourists. Given the rather diverse nature of demand, the hospitality industry is also looking at creating adequate products to service the varied tourist requirements. With the support and initiatives by the governments at various levels, the hospitality sector is moving towards comprehensive growth"

NCR, with a total supply of 17,500 rooms, is expected to see the highest fresh hotel room supply in five years. Mumbai (10,200) and Bangalore (9,400) will also see significant addition to the existing inventories in the city. The addition of new inventory will be concentrated in the potential growth areas – especially around airports, commercial growth corridors, industrial corridors and SEZs. These micro markets emerged as a result of business centres that were created in these cities due to growth in

IT/ITeS, trade and commerce.

TABLE 1(B).13:

Hotel Supply

Hotel Supply (No of rooms)			
City Wise	H1-2012	H2-2012	Upcoming
Bengaluru	400	3,800	9,400
Chennai	160	2,200	5,150
Hyderabad	430	160	3,720
Kolkata	0	150	4,500
Mumbai	300	1,540	10,200
NCR	830	5,000	17,550
Total	2,120	12,850	50,520

Source: Cushman & Wakefield research

The top six cites witnessed an Average Occupancy (AO) of 58 per cent with an Average Room Rate (ARR) of INR 5,400 in H1 2012. The current averages record a marginal decline of 4 per cent in AOR and 5 per cent in ARR over the average of 2011 (full year) performance. Chennai recorded the highest Average Occupancy Rates (AOR) of 64 per cent for H1 2012, followed by Mumbai (61 per cent) and Kolkata (60 per cent). All the cities witnessed only a marginal drop in AOR when compared to the previous year 2011. Mumbai and Kolkata saw the maximum dip in AOR.

A decline in AOR in popular destinations was due to a number of factors but primarily due to addition of supply in major cities in H1 2012. On the other hand, a moderate slowdown in global economies led many corporations to curtail travel, while individual travelers have also been cautious due to fiscal uncertainties. Some other factors that have contributed to lower AOR are the advancements in technologies, which make real time correspondence faster, easier and more cost effective and increase connectivity that ensure lesser hours of stay per visit. A corresponding decline in ARR was noticed as hotels tried to ensure occupancy even at a moderately lower cost. Healthy competition in many of the cities is leading hotels to create monetarily attractive packages for potential visitors.

In H1, 2012 Mumbai, recorded the highest ARR of INR 6,400, followed by NCR INR 6,280 and Bengaluru INR 4,915. While Chennai and Hyderabad witnessed marginal increase in ARR, all other cities saw the rates as wither stable or softening over 2011.

TABLE 1(B).14:

City wise Average Occupancy Rate (AOR)

City Wise	Average Occupancy Rate (AOR)	
	2011	**H1-2012**
Bengaluru	59 per cent	57 per cent
Chennai	67 per cent	64 per cent
Hyderabad	54 per cent	53 per cent
Kolkata	66 per cent	60 per cent

Mumbai	67 per cent	61 per cent
NCR	63 per cent	58 per cent
Average/Total	62 per cent	58 per cent

Source: Cushman & Wakefield research

TABLE 1(B).15:

City wise Average Room Rate (ARR)

City Wise	Average Room Rate (ARR)	
	2011	H1-2012
Bengaluru	5,740	4,915
Chennai	4,700	4,900
Hyderabad	3,790	3,830
Kolkata	4,900	4,770
Mumbai	6,395	6,400
NCR	6,555	6,280
Average/Total	5,723	5,444

Source: Cushman & Wakefield research

Akshay, added, "Occupancy rates may see an upward trend in the second half of 2012 keeping ARRs steady. However, since there is a substantial supply that is expected to enter the market over the new few years, the pressure on occupancy rate and ARRs will continue. The phasing of the new inventory and gradual growth in the demand for hotels will help keep the rates at modest levels across the country. However going forward we expect ARRs to improve in the next 12- 18 months on account of stability in economy and expected growth in tourism in India. Also with more and more international brands operating in the country, the market will move towards being more organised and standardisation of process including cost per room night."

Source: Friday, September 21, 2012, 13:00 Hrs [IST]

By HBI Staff | Mumbai

Tourism outlay to increase three-fold in 12th Five Year Plan period

According to Subodh Kant Sahai, Minister for Tourism, Government of India, expenditure for implementing tourism plans will see a three-fold increase in the 12th Five Year Plan period (2012-17), compared with the 11th Plan period. The Planning Commission of India has sanctioned a plan outlay of Rs 16,000 crore for tourism, versus Rs 5,156 crore in the previous period. Speaking at the Golden Jubilee Celebrations of Institute of Hotel Management (IHM) Pusa, New Delhi, Sahai said that the increased allocation was an indicator of the changing outlook of the government towards the tourism sector. He said that the ministry will soon convene a meeting of the National Tourism Advisory Council (NTAC) to chart plans for the next five years.

In the proposals submitted to the Planning Commission, the ministry had sought an increased allocation to undertake major tourism development projects, including 35 new destinations/tourism circuits/tourism cities in the pattern of the Jawaharlal Nehru National Urban Renewal Mission (JNNURM) or the Delhi-Mumbai Industrial Corridor, 20 new tourism parks around major tourism destinations to increase overnights by visitors, creation of Rural Tourism clusters by combining villages with unique art, craft, etc. The Ministry of Tourism, Government of India envisages achieving foreign tourism arrivals of 11.24 million by the end of the 12th Five Year Plan period.

Source: Saturday, September 15, 2012, 14:00 Hrs [IST]

By P Krishna Kumar | New Delhi

Hotel Price Index reveals rise in hotel prices globally

For the first time in five years, travellers paid more on average for their hotel rooms during the first six months of 2012 in all parts of the world, according to the latest Hotel Price Index report by Hotels.com. The global four per cent rise, compared to the same period the year before, demonstrated that the economic recovery in the hotel industry was well-established.

The index stood at 108 for this period meaning that, despite the latest increase, hotel prices in general were still considerably lower than in the first half of 2007 when the HPI was at its peak of 119.

During the first six months of 2012, prices rose across the board with Pacific rates up 6 per cent, North America up 5 per cent and Asia up 4 per cent while Latin America as well as Europe and the Middle East experienced a slower trajectory, up one per cent.

David Roche, President, Hotels.com, said, "The hotel industry bounced back in the first half of this year from a number of natural and political crises in 2011 and it is encouraging to see growth in the sector. While initially it may not seem good news for consumers, hotel prices are still only around their 2005 level, representing great value for travellers when both wages and other prices have risen considerably."

Following the turmoil of the Arab Spring in early 2011, confidence returned to much of the Middle East and North Africa and hotel prices rose accordingly.

In India, the overall rate rose 12 per cent following a surge in demand from domestic travellers as overseas destinations became more expensive but the country remained the destination with the lowest rates in the HPI. Japanese began to travel again after the turbulence of the earthquake, tsunami and nuclear disaster in March 2011 but there were other factors at play here as well. The significant increase in the number of Chinese international travellers helped to drive rates higher and expansion by the region's low cost carriers, such as Peach Aviation and Scoot, also boosted travel.

In the USA, increasing business travel combined with higher consumer spending meant hotels were busier with less need for discounting. In the Pacific, the resources boom in Australia meant that space was at a premium, particularly in Western Australia with international business visitors vying with mining executives for rooms.

Although rates rose as a whole in Europe, the results showed a mixed picture. One of the areas where prices dropped was in parts of the Eurozone where falling consumer confidence and spending power led to lower occupancy in the major cities and holiday hotspots.

Source: Friday, September 07, 2012, 10:00 Hrs [IST]

By HBI Staff | Mumbai

STR Global, Horwath HTL analyse hotel performance in India from Jan-June 2012

STR Global and Horwath HTL in their latest India Market Hotel Review presented the analysis of hotel performance in India from Jan to June 2012. The dry business sentiments (monsoon included) affecting India have carried through to the hotel sector in the first six months of 2012 (H1 2012). Although 2012 occupancies at the mid-year level are higher than 59.9 per cent achieved in calendar year 2011, the H1 2012 Average Daily Rate (ADR) and Revenue PerAvailable Room (RevPAR) are lower than calendar year 2011 by 4.4 per cent and 3.8 per cent respectively.

Some of the standout features from the performance in H1 2012 stated that Kolkata is the only city (among leading markets) reporting growth in occupancy, ADR and RevPAR in H1 2012, compared to H1 2011; Pune has reported sharp improvement in occupancy by 8.2 pts; while ADR declined by 11.1 per cent, Pune is only one of the three major markets that enjoyed RevPAR growth in H1 2012 compared to H1 2011; Goa enjoyed occupancy growth of 1.5 pts, which was somewhat diluted due to 0.8 per cent ADR decline leading to a nominal RevPAR growth of 1.1 per cent; Delhi NCR and Mumbai suffered 9.4 per cent and 6 per cent RevPAR decline respectively, due to decline in both occupancy and ADR.

According to the report, however, Mumbai is the only city in India with H1 2012 ADR above Rs 8,000 and RevPAR above Rs 5,000. Bengaluru has suffered severely with occupancy drop of 6.3 pts and RevPAR decline of 20.4 per cent in the relevant comparable periods. Clearly, the absorption of new supply is slow and city centre hotels are hurting due to newer and more efficiently priced products in business area micro markets. However, it must also be recognised that Bengaluru has the widest spread of hotels across segments, including mid-market and budget products.

Other findings explained that Chennai is the only other market that has suffered double digit decline in RevPAR in H1 2012; with substantial supply still to come on line the present hurt would likely become more painful. On the other hand, Jaipur and Hyderabad witnessed nominal occupancy growth in H1 2012, compared to H1 2011; while RevPAR declined in these markets; the extent of decline was lower than the national average.

Source: Sunday, September 23, 2012, 17:00 Hrs [IST]

By HBI Staff | Mumbai

The world's biggest travel spenders

With demand for international tourism growing and the number of tourist arrivals reaching 983 million worldwide, up from 940 million in 2010 tourism has experienced continued expansion and diversification, becoming one of the largest and fastest-growing economic sectors in the world.

The UNWTO's report on 2012 tourism highlights gives the list of the countries that invest the most in the tourism sector. India was the fastest growing source market among the top 50 spenders with a 33% increase, moving up two places to 22nd in the ranking.

Gallery View: The world's biggest travel spenders

1. Around $50 billion is spent by the United Kingdom for tourism and the country saw 29 million tourists. The recently concluded Olympics unfortunately did not do wonders for the country's tourism. 3 million tourists visited the UK in August, less from 3.15 million last year.

   Around $50 billion is spent by the United Kingdom for tourism and the country saw 29 million tourists. The recently concluded Olympics unfortunately did not do wonders for the country's tourism. 3 million tourists visited the UK in August, less from 3.15 million last year.

2. With its main attractions such as the Eiffel Tower and charming sidewalk cafés, the country stands fifth in the international tourist spenders list with $41.7 billion. However, the country sees the highest number of tourists, an almost staggering 80 million tourists!

With its main attractions such as the Eiffel Tower and charming sidewalk cafés, the country stands fifth in the international tourist spenders list with $41.7 billion. However, the country sees the highest number of tourists, an almost staggering 80 million tourists!

3. Another representative from North America, Canada spends $33 billion on tourism and sees around 15 million tourists. The country is also looking to reduce the tax burden on the aviation industry to attract more foreign tourists especially from the BRIC countries.

Another representative from North America, Canada spends $33 billion on tourism and sees around 15 million tourists. The country is also looking to reduce the tax burden on the aviation industry to attract more foreign tourists especially from the BRIC countries.

4. The Russian Federation spends around $32 billion on tourism and sees 22 million tourists. Since the Soviet times, the tourism sector has seen a lot of growth and the country is home to 23 World Heritage Sites such as Lake Baikal, Moscow Kremlin, Red Square.

5. The Russian Federation spends around $32 billion on tourism and sees 22 million tourists. Since the Soviet times, the tourism sector has seen a lot of growth and the country is home to 23 World Heritage Sites such as Lake Baikal, Moscow Kremlin, Red Square.

6. With the famed Colosseum and a country known for its food, Italy emerges as the eigth highest spender with $28 billion and sees 46 million tourists. Italy

contains the most number of World Heritage Sites than any other country. With the famed Colosseum and a country known for its food, Italy emerges as the eigth highest spender with $28 billion and sees 46 million tourists. Italy contains the most number of World Heritage Sites than any other country.

7. $27 billion was spent by Japan in 2011 and compared to other countries in the list sees a meager 6 million tourists. Hot springs are extremely famous in this country and are one of the main draws apart from its network of hotels.

8. Australia finishes last in this list with a tourism expenditure of $26.9 billion and tourist arrivals of 5 million. In 2010-11, the tourism sector contributed around $95 million a day to the Australian economy. The Sydney Gay and Lesbian Mardi Gras, an annual event usually attracts thousands of international tourists.

9. India with its Incredible India tourism campaigns sees 6 million tourist arrivals and is the largest tourism destination in the sub-region of Asia Pacific. A total of $17 billion was spent on tourism. The sector is also expected to create 78 jobs per million rupees of investment.

Source: UNWTO Tourism Highlights 2012 Edition

TOURISM AND HOTEL INDUSTRY: S.W.O.T ANALYSIS: (INDIA)

The specific strength and weakness of the product in relation to the market segments identified are analyzed along with the existing opportunities and threats. A typical SWOT analysis matrix in case of India in reaction to competitive destinations is as under:-

There are various environmental forces influence the tourism industry. The other aspect of this industry is that it is heavily dependent on a set of other industries who are in turn dependant on the tourist flow for their business. This combination of various industries has to work as one to increase the tourist's traffic of the country. This set of industries takes care of the activities that support tourism industry is:

- **The Hotel Industry**
- **Airlines**
- **The Railways**
- **Road Networks**
- **The Tour Operators**
- **The Government**

These facilities decide the status of a place in a tourist's portfolio. They on one hand attract tourists to a particular destination and on the other act as a major de-motivating factor if they are unable to fulfill the expectations of the visitors. So the major bottlenecks to this industry are looked into on a priority basis.

Given below is the SWOT analysis of the **Tourism industry** in India.

STRENGTHS:

- India's geographical location is a culmination of forests, deserts, and mountains and beaches.
- Diversity of culture i.e. a blend of various civilizations and their traditions.
- A wealth of archeological sites and historical monuments.
- Rich culture heritage and colorful festivals.
- Scenic beauty of the country draws tourists from far off places.
- Terrain is ideally suited for various adventure activities.
- Well known Indian hospitality.

WEAKNESSES

- A xenophobic attitude among certain sections of the people.
- No proper marketing of India tourism abroad.
- Foreigners still think of India as a land of snake charmers.
- Inadequate infrastructure to match the expectation.

- Restrictive Airline Policy of the Government of India.
- Overcrowding of popular tourist centers.
- Inadequate marketing and information channels.
- Some places are inaccessible, especially in winter

OPPORTUNITIES

- More proactive role from the government of India in terms of framing policies. Allowing entry of more multinational companies into the country giving us a global perspective.
- As well as growth of domestic tourism is one of the factors of the development of the tourism industry.
- GOI is giving special attention to certain regions like Northeast India.
- Asian Development Bank is preparing a Sub-Regional Plan for development of tourism in India.
- Potential for private sector's investment in tourism projects.
- Availability of high quality human resource.

THREATS

- Economic conditions and political turmoil in other countries affects tourism.
- Aggressive strategies adopted by other countries like Australia, Singapore in promoting their tourism affects Indian tourism.
- Strong Competition within states of India and abroad.
- Terrorism is a major setback of the region.
- Disorganized tourism development.
- Environmental factors also impose a threat

SWOT ANALYSIS; HOTEL INDUSTRY

Hotels form one of the most important support service that affect the arrival of tourist to a country. The major players in the industry are Indian Hotels Company Ltd (IHCL) operating under the Taj brand, the Oberoi, Welcome Group of Hotels, Hotel Leela Venture and the Ashoka chain of hotels, owned and operated by the Indian Tourism Development Corporation (ITDC).

There are around 1000 classified hotels and the total room availability is pegged at 97,000 rooms. Hotels are classified into six categories according to the star rating assigned by the Department of Tourism. These range from One star to Five star deluxe depending upon size and amenities. About 30% of the rooms fall under the 5-star deluxe categories.

To find out the present status of this industry strength, weakness opportunity and threat (SWOT) analysis is mental. This will help us in understanding this industry and also identify the weak spots.

STRENGTHS

- A very wide variety of hotels is present in the country that can fulfill the demand of the tourists.
- There are international players in the market such as Taj and Oberoi & International Chains. Thus, the needs of the international tourists travellers are met while they are on a visit to India.
- Manpower costs in the Indian hotel industry is one of the lowest in the world. This provides better margins for Indian hotel industry.
- India offers a readymade tourist destination with the resources it has. Thus the magnet to pull customers already exists and has potential grow.

WEAKNESSES

- The cost of land in India is high at 50% of total project cost as against 15% abroad. This acts as a major deterrent to the Indian hotel industry.

- The hotel industry in India is heavily staffed. This can be gauged from the facts that while Indian hotel companies have a staff to room ratio of 3:1, this ratio is 1:1 for international hotel companies.

- High tax structure in the industry makes the industry worse off than its international equivalent. In India the expenditure tax, luxury tax and sales tax inflate the hotel bill by over 30%. Effective tax in the South East Asian countries works out to only 4-5%.

- Only 97,000 hotel rooms are available in India today, which is less than the Bangkok hotel capacity.

- The services currently offered by the hotels in India are only limited value added services. It is not comparable to the existing world standards.

OPPORTUNITIES

- Demand between the national and the inbound tourists can be easily managed due to difference in the period of holidays. For international tourists the peak season for arrival is between September to March when the climatic conditions are suitable where as the national tourist waits for school holidays, generally the summer months.

- In the long-term the hotel industry in India has latent potential for growth. This is because India is an ideal destination for tourists as it is the only country with the most diverse topography. For India, the inbound tourists are a mere 0.49% of the global figures. This number is expected to increase at a phenomenal rate thus pushing up the demand for the hotel industry.

- Unique experience in heritage hotels.

THREATS

- Guest houses, serviced apartments and home-stays replace the hotels. This is a growing trend in the west and is now catching up in India also, thus diverting the hotel traffic.

- Political turbulence in the area reduces tourist traffic and thus the business of the hotels. In India examples of the same are Insurgency in Jammu Kashmir and the Kargil war.

- Changing trends in the west demand similar changes in India, which here are difficult to implement due to high project costs.

- The economic conditions of a country have a direct impact on the earnings in hotel industry. Lack of training man power in the hotel industry.

CHAPTER 1.2

LITERATURE REVIEW

Service quality is a way to manage business processes in order to ensure total satisfaction to the customer on all levels (internal and external). It is an approach that leads to an increase of competitiveness, effectiveness and flexibility of the entire company. Benefits arising from a high quality are reflected in a more competitive positioning on the market, but also in a better business result. This statement can be proved by measuring the increase of profitability and market share. Various researches show a direct connection between the level of quality of goods and services and their financial performances. As a matter of fact, it was observed that all indicators of success of a company, like market share, return on investments, property turnover coefficient, and show significantly more value in companies with a higher level of goods and services.

The efficiency of the whole system is possible only if we monitor and analyze the demands of the customers, as well as define and control the process and implement constant improvements. Quality is a complex term, made up of several elements and criteria. All quality elements or criteria are equally important in order to obtain one hundred percent quality. If only one element of quality is missing, the complete quality of product or service is impossible to obtain.

Besides the mentioned general elements of quality, the product or services have to satisfy specific elements of quality, according to the demands of the profession in their pertaining activity. Today quality is the result of growing and increasingly diverse needs of the consumers, along with a highly increasing competition, market globalization and the development of modern technology.

Problems in service quality measurement arise from a lack of clear and measurable parameters for the determination of quality. It is not the cases with product quality since products have specific and measurable indicators like durability, number of defective products and similar, which make it relatively easy to determine the level of quality. Today quality is the result of growing and increasingly diverse needs of the consumers, along with a highly increasing competition, market globalization and the development of modern technology.

The literature here is being discussed within four broad sections.

The first section contains **hotel industry** specific literature relating to the characteristics of the industry, its structure and competitive forces.

 The second continues with the criterion **Service**.

The third section relates to **service quality**.

The final section relates to **service quality measurement**.

This structure allows comparison of research in a broader context with that in the narrower hospitality field allowing a clearer identification of the gaps in the literature that contribute to the research questions.

THE HOTEL INDUSTRY

Several scholars have viewed services as deeds, performances, activities or processes. As Parasuraman (1985) noted, services are behavioral entities which are intangible, perishable, inseparable, and heterogeneous. These attributes imply that services cannot be accurately measured and maintained by a firm (Harvey, 1998). The key concern arising here is that management has to ensure that the overall quality of service maximizes benefits while minimizing cost.

Grönroos (1984) felt that service quality could be further divided into technical quality and functional quality, which he viewed as fundamentally different. Technical quality answers what the consumer obtains and functional quality answers how the consumer obtains it. Actually, functional quality can only be recognized subjectively; therefore, obviously functional quality cannot be evaluated objectively like technical quality (Cheng-Nan, Shueh-Chin (2002). In other words, technical quality is the practical result of service and functional quality indicates the process of carrying out the service (Grönroos, 1990).

Service quality make-up does not just involve the results but includes the methods and procedures used to convey the service. Many researchers support this notion (Bolton and Drew, 1991; Weng, 1994).

Service Quality and Customer Satisfaction
Gabbie and O'Neill (1996) observed that in today's hospitality environment, the true measure of company success lies in an organization's ability to satisfy customers continually. Increasingly customers are demanding value for money in terms of both price and the quality of product/service being offered. In order to ensure market success, hospitality organizations of all types are being forced to stand back and take a long, hard look at the way they are currently doing business. As such, failure by management to interpret customer desires accurately can result in loss of business and possible bankruptcy for some.

There has been some confusion regarding the differences between service quality and satisfaction (Storbacka, Strandvik, and Grönroos (1984). Satisfaction would, according to Liljander and Strandvik (1994), refer to an insider perspective, the customer's own experiences of a service where the outcome has been evaluated in terms of what value was received, in other words what the customer had to give to get something. According to Jaccard, J., & King, G. W. (1977), satisfaction is an evaluation that an 'experience was at least as good as it was perceived to be'. One way to achieve strong relationships and, thus, long relationships is to ensure that customers are satisfied. The proposition is that dissatisfied customers will defect; the relationship ends. Several researchers have proposed that this is a simplification of the matter (Zeithaml, et al., 1993). Customers seem to have a zone of tolerance, which according to Zeithaml, et al., (1993) can be defined as the difference between an adequate and a desired level of service. According to Kennedy and Thirkell (1998), customers are prepared to absorb some unfavorable evaluations before expressing them in terms of net dissatisfaction.

The global hotel industry is a major component of the travel and tourism industry, generating over US$247 billion in 1995 (Olsen, 1996). It is an extensive industry defined as "a set of lodging firms, including motels, in competition, and producing goods and services of a like function and nature" (Go and Pine 1995 pg 25).
A hotel, within this industry, is defined as "any facility that regularly (or occasionally) provides overnight accommodations" (Olsen 1996, pg 20).

The hotel industry is highly complex in that there are several independent but competing elements (hotels, resorts, motels, guest-houses etc.) within the industry (Go & Pine, 1995; Littlejohn, 2003). Each element has internal quality classifications (one star to five star or economy to luxury) and diverse customer groups (business, leisure & convention travellers) (Jones, 2002; Lewis et al., 1995). In addition to the diversity within the industry, we must note the complexity of the operating environment is extended for the multinational hotel industry with "the unique challenge of competing in three business environments: international, national and local" (Olsen 1996, pg 29).

According to the International Hotel Association report 'Into the New Millennium' (Olsen 1996) the global hotel industry comprised 307,683 hotels with 11,333,199 bedrooms in 1995. The hotel industry has experienced significant growth over the last thirty years (Go & Pine, 1995; Olsen, 1996) with, in particular, a growth in the number of bedrooms worldwide by over twenty five percent in the period from 1990 to 1998 (Littlejohn, 2003).

There is some consensus that similar increases occurred in the previous decade (Go & Pine, 1995). Weaver and Oh (1993) commented that many hotel companies capitalised on the growth and expansion trends that followed World War II, especially in the more developed nations, such as the USA and some of the countries in Europe. In more recent times the expansion trends of the hotel companies have transferred to the less developed and developing countries (Olsen, 1996).

The hotel industry is a highly complex industry (Olsen, 1996) that contains many sub-sections, yet also competes at a broader level within specific geographic areas (Lewis et al., 1995). At the product level, the hotel industry is categorised by hotel quality and style. For example, most consumers are familiar with the star quality ratings and the slightly broader categorisations of luxury, first class, mid-range and economy, but within these categorizations there are also several types of hotel such as business or leisure hotels, apartment or all-suite hotels (Lewis et al., 1995; Littlejohn, 2003). Equally, the location of a hotel, such as city outskirts, seaside, rural or roadside also provides a reasonable segmentation of hotels (Olsen, 1996).

In general a first class hotel competes with another first class hotel, but within any given geographic area a first class hotel may also compete with a luxury, mid-range or economy hotel depending on the range of hotels available at the destination (Lewis et al., 1995). The structure is also made complex by a separation of ownership and management, with few industries reflecting the range of stakeholders commonplace in the hotel industry that include franchisors, management firms and owners (Dube & Renaghan, 1999c; Littlejohn, 2003).

Competition within the Hotel Industry
The hotel industry is changing, reflecting higher levels of concentration and competition (Go & Pine, 1995; Littlejohn, 2003; Olsen, 1996). The emergence, post WWII, of large

hotel groups operating internationally has fundamentally changed the hotel industry from a fragmented industry with most hotels individually owned, to one dominated by large groups (Littlejohn, 2003; Olsen, 1996).

This process of change and consolidation is continuing and a more internationalised and concentrated industry is expected to develop (Go and Pine 1995, Olsen 1996). The structure of an industry and the concentration of firms within that industry determines the behaviour of participating organisations (Needham, 1978). The hotel industry has historically been considered fragmented, as the industry level of concentration is perceived as low (Littlejohn, 2003).

The assumption that the level of concentration is low derives from two major reasons. First, the diversity within the industry is high. Second, there is wide ranging ownership with many hotel companies only owning one or a small number of properties (Littlejohn, 2003).

However it may be argued that the industry has consolidated over recent years. According to figures derived from the International Hotel Association report (Olsen, 1996), the top twenty hotel companies only controlled 6.45 per cent of the world hotel stock at that time, indicating a low level of concentration. However in terms of the number of bedrooms, the top twenty hotel companies controlled 23.44 per cent of the total, thereby providing a different impression. Littlejohn (2003) supports this, citing Todd and Mather (2002), who suggest that less than 20 per cent of European hotels belong to branded chains, whilst also citing statistics that show a growth in rooms belonging to the top twenty hotel companies from 1.8 million to 3.6 million in the period from 1990 to 2001. The level of concentration is thus determined by the term of measurement, hotel properties or hotel rooms, and although the level of concentration is still low in comparison with many other industries, it is far higher than initially indicated. These figures, however, give an inaccurate perception of the levels of concentration and competitive rivalry that exist within certain discrete sectors of the industry. The hotel industry includes luxury, first class, mid-range, and economy hotels, high quality and standard motels as well as other forms of accommodation, such as caravan parks, serviced apartments and guesthouses. It is in this context, at the industry level, that the hotel industry may be seen as fragmented, but in reality the industry comprises several sub-industries, some of which show very different structural characteristics.

The majority of the hotels owned by the top twenty hotel companies would be found within certain discreet sectors of the industry, such as the higher priced first class and luxury sectors, and the economy sectors, and within these sectors the levels of concentration would be much higher (Jones, 2002).

These sectors, dominated by the large hotel groups, tend to have high levels of competitive rivalry. The level of competitive rivalry positively correlates with the following characteristics, all prevalent in these sectors of the hotel industry: high levels of concentration, high entry barriers, homogeneous products, high cross elasticity, high fixed costs and where there is excess capacity (Johnson & Scholes, 2002). Additional factors, also prevalent in the hotel industry that exacerbate the levels of competitive rivalry are low buyer loyalty and low switching costs (Skogland & Siguaw, 2004), which lead to a willingness to switch between brands. For the hotel industry, within an individual quality sector, there is a lack of sources of competitive advantage at the group level as there are limited sources of product differentiation or cost advantage (Bowen & Shoemaker, 1998; Kandampully & Suhartanto, 2000; Lewis et al., 1995).

Differentiation arises from a buyer perspective and, in general, within a hotel quality grading, there is little differentiation, from the consumer's perspective, between hotels of any given standard (Bowen & Shoemaker, 1998; Kandampully & Suhartanto, 2000).

As an example of the limited differentiation, hotel general managers from a luxury brand in Asia were shown photographs of hotel rooms from their own brand, and three competitors, with most of the managers being unable to identify any of the rooms including their own (Bowen & Shoemaker, 1998).

Individual properties can hold competitive advantage for many reasons, including tangible aspects such as location, physical attributes or facilities, as well as intangible aspects related to service issues or specific characteristics (Lewis et al., 1995). At a group level, within a quality classification, the competitive advantage that can derive from the uniqueness available to a single hotel is not available and, therefore, the development and management of strong brands is seen as a key driver of success in the face of highly competitive markets, and low product differentiation (Delgado-Ballester & Munuera-Alemán, 2000; Jiang, Dev & Rao, 2002). Tepeci (1999 pg 223) suggests that as a mature industry, with "rising international competition, slower growth rates, decreased population growth and oversupplied and mature markets", the hotel industry needs to pursue market share rather than market growth strategies with consumer loyalty being paramount to a successful strategy.

In summary the hotel industry provides a significant economic and employment contribution to the Indian and global economies. The industry has seen a long period of growth and consolidation that has fundamentally changed the competitive climate, particularly in discrete sectors such as the first class and luxury sectors, those chosen for this study. These sectors, whilst still showing comparatively low levels of concentration, are dominated by the major hotel groups. But, due to a lack of physical product differentiation, these groups seek to rely on brand attitudes as a source of competitive advantage.

SERVICE

What is Service?

"Anything useful, such as maintenance, supplies installation, repairs, etc, provided by a dealer or manufacturer for people who have bought things from him." Two decades ago, people defined service as mentioned above. According to Webster's New 20th Century Dictionary (second edition). But today we believe this definition is not sufficient to cover what service means. Today it is more appropriate to define service as "useful labor that does not produce a tangible commodity" in a customer-oriented point of view. (Davidoff, 1994)

Harris (2000) noted customer service is anything we do for the customer that enhances the customer experience. Customers have varying ideas of what they expect from customer interaction. No matter how accurately we see our definition of customer service, we still have to live up to what our customer thinks that customer service is. The customer's satisfaction is the goal to attain in service industry.

How Service Differs from Manufacturing

From a manufacturing standpoint money is the most important capital, a means of expansion and growth. Davidoff (1994) mentioned manufacturing companies have a strong financial orientation. From a service standpoint, people are the most important capital. They represent not only a company's major investment, but also its chief asset. Employees and their professional growth are more important than financial capital in determining the extent of company growth. People are the biggest competitive edge that a service company has. No matter how much money the company invests or how well a facility is built, the employees will ultimately determine success because quality, productivity and consistency are determined by factors like sensitivity, responsiveness, helpfulness, friendliness, good instincts, courtesy, teamwork, risk-taking, initiative, flair, self-confidence, innovation and creativity. So in service industry, the approach to human resource management must be designed to create an environment that will allow these factors to grow and develop.

Involved customers can influence the treatment of subsequent customers by the effect they have on service providers. Because of these major differences, in quality service we must become cognizant of what a process is and how variation affects the quality of service such as employees' attitude, knowledge and skill of decision making and problem-solving. Stamatis (1996) said the consequences of these characteristics are that involved customers can rush, slow down, disrupt, and alter production processes. In addition, according to Davidoff (1994) we can find out what is different between a service and a retail product. For many years, business treated services about the same as they treated any retail goods. In the 1970s, however, a new view emerged-one that understands that service is distinctly different from manufacturing and retail.

In the world of hotel customer service, where the norm is to perform "beyond the call of duty" (Staroba, 1992), it is necessary to recognize the diversity of services that are provided and that should be provided to hotel guests. Hospitality service quality is a multi-attribute construct (Richard & Allaway, 1993). Hoteliers would agree that the basics – room, food, and prompt and friendly service – are just a starting point, not the goal of service. Hotel companies benefit greatly from genuine attempts to identify, interpret and respond to the feelings and needs of their customers (Anonymous, 1993). Satisfaction with a lodging property occurs only when the hotel is organized to provide quality service for each and every guest. When certain intangible amenities exist, it indicates that the hotel is focused on creating a consistent experience (Roderick, 1996).

The Importance of Customer Service

Return business indicates the best service. As characteristics of service, service cannot be separate from customer in service industry. Customers and service are an obvious requirement for doing business. Harris (2000) mentions one of the most effective and least expensive ways to market a business is through excellent customer service. The importance of customer service is at an all-time high. Many services require personal interactions between customers and the firm's employees, and these interactions strongly influence the customers' perception of service quality (Rust, Zahorik, & Keiningham, 1995) For instance, a person's stay at hotel can be greatly affected by the friendliness, knowledgeability, and helpfulness of the hotel staff. One's impression of the hotel and willingness to return are determined to a large extent by the brief encounters with the front desk staff, bell person, housekeeping staff, restaurant staff.

Customer service is the positive element that keeps current business coming back. Today, customers are much more sophisticated than they were ten years ago. Businesses realize that providing a service alone is not enough in today's competitive economic environment. They are informed about how products should perform and know that if they are dissatisfied with the service that they receive, someone else probably sells the product and will provide better service. Even they may also expect that expressing their unhappiness with a situation will elicit a positive result to other place. (Harris, 2000) In high competitive industry, customer who is not satisfied with staying at hotel, they simply won't return and change their hotel next time. Therefore, management faces a tremendous challenge in improving the service by selecting and training all of these employees to do their jobs well, and perhaps even more important in motivating them to provide good service to customers.

SERVICE QUALITY

Service quality in the hotel industry has been examined in a number of studies (Chang et al., 2002; Sargeant & Mohamad, 1999; Tsang & Qu, 2000) and there are a number of models that conceptualise the construct of service quality (e.g. Gronroos, 2001; Bienstock, Mentzer, & Bird, 1997; Parasuraman, Zeithaml, & Berry, 1988; Garvin, 1987). More recently researchers are concerned with the management of services (Rowley & Richardson, 2000) whilst others focus on why best practice does not work (Lockyer & Scholarios, 2004). Some consider measurement and the use of

SERVQUAL in hotels in Northern Ireland (Gabbie & O'Neill, 1997), whilst Chang et al. (2002) consider its use in Korean hotels. Chu (2002) uses SERVQUAL and the regression models and finds similarity between both approaches. Recent UK research focuses on service management issues (Nolan, 2002) and on the use of technology (Buick, 2003). However, comparative research across the Scottish hotel sector is less common, other than in more generic reports.

Service quality and its determinants
There is a lack of consensus about the construct of service quality (Johnston, 1995). The most common approach is that of the disconfirmation paradigm (Robledo, 2001) which asserts that quality can be defined as the gap between customers' expectations and perceptions Parasuraman, Zeithaml, & Berry, 1994). These researchers proposed a conceptual framework capturing the dimensions utilised by customers when evaluating service quality. The dimensions were then applied to a gap model (SERVQUAL), where customers compared prior expectations of service provision with post experience perceptions (Parasuraman, Zeithaml, & Berry, 1985; Parasurman et al., 1988). Criticism of the gap model (Cronin & Taylor, 1994) led to the emergence of the derived importance approach which links customer satisfaction to service quality (Bolton & Drew, 1994). Rather than collect ratings of perceived importance associated with service dimensions, regression models identify significant drivers of satisfaction. This precipitated the development of SERVPERF (Cronin & Taylor, 1994) and Normed Quality models (Teas, 1993). In a study of Hong Kong hotels, Chu (2002) suggests that the derived importance model is the more statistically reliable approach. Nevertheless, there is still wide support for both approaches. There is agreement that the problems involved in addressing service quality management are in part a reflection of the intangible, simultaneous, non-standardised and perishable nature of services (Harris & Harrington, 2000). The characteristics of services and their relationship to service quality are also difficult to clarify (Soteriou & Chase, 1998). The hotel sector faces manufacturing problems in providing high quality products and service delivery problems in providing high quality services (Keating & Harrington, 2002). The delivery of hotel services involves high contact encounters with significant interaction among

customers, staff and facilities (Lovelock & Wright, 1999). Variability is inherent (and in some cases desirable) in service delivery. The challenge for management is to balance the need for routine and standardisation with the need to treat customers as individuals. Excellent companies know that positive employee attitudes promotes stronger customer loyalty, thus companies must attract the best employees with a long-term career focus (Kotler & Keller, 2006).

Additionally, in a high contact setting, the physical evidence (tangibles) gives strong clues as to the quality of the service provider by communicating a message to the customer about the establishment before and during the encounter, and strongly influences the evaluation of the overall experience (Lovelock & Wright, 1999).

There is consensus that the quality of the service encounter is critical to business success or failure and that service quality is rarely concerned with a single aspect of service but with the whole service package (Berry, Carbone, & Haechel, 2002). Indeed service quality in a tourism context has been viewed mostly as the quality of the opportunities available at a destination and is considered to be related to a tourist's quality of experience (Crompton & Love, 1995). Underpinning our understanding of service quality is an array of determinants or dimensions which are critical for service management as these are essential to specify, measure, control and improve customer perceived service (Johnston, 1995). There is debate over the number and actual determinants of service quality. Garvin (1987) identifies eight determinants; performance, features, reliability, conformance, durability, serviceability, aesthetics and perceived quality. Parasuraman et al. (1985) identified ten which were subsequently collapsed into five (Parasuraman et al., 1988); tangibles, reliability, responsiveness, assurance and empathy. Walker (1990) identifies product reliability, a quality environment and delivery systems that work together with good personal service, whilst Johnston, Sivestro, Fitzgerald, and Voss (1990) signal that there are as many as eighteen determinants. Subsequently, Johnston (1995) argues that researchers have not distinguished between the effect of determinants in the creation of satisfaction or dissatisfaction.

Customer satisfaction and Service Quality delivery

The relationship between service quality and satisfaction has attracted much research in recent years (Johnston, 1995, 2004; Qu et al., 2000). There is broad consensus that service quality and customer (visitor) satisfaction is different constructs but little agreement on the nature of their relationship although both influence visitors' future destination selection intentions (Tian-Cole & Crompton, 2003). This is important to Scotland as it tries to grow tourism and become a leading international destination by 2015. Service quality is an overall evaluation of the destination and satisfaction is concerned with the overall evaluation of the experience at the destination (Tian-Cole & Crompton, 2003). Early work on satisfaction and dissatisfaction treated (dis)satisfaction as a two state construct (e.g. angry or not angry) whilst recently satisfaction is conceptualised as a continuum often expressed in terms of emotions (Johnston, 2004). However the emotional basis for the satisfaction response is not well documented (Oliver, 1997).

Notwithstanding, recent research suggests that emotions play a major role in perceived levels of service quality and satisfaction (Dube & Menon, 1998). These researchers linked feelings of anger and frustration to decreases in dissatisfaction and emotions such as happiness to increases in satisfaction. Excellent service results in positive feelings of 'delight' at one end of this emotional spectrum. In the past many businesses have been satisfied with meeting perceptions of customers' 'adequate' expectations, whereas nowadays the emphasis is on customer satisfaction (Fisk, 2002). In the future more businesses will be concerned with achieving customer 'delight' because satisfying customers is not enough to retain them (Schneider & Bowen, 1999). Whilst many businesses continue to promise exceptional service, and focus on doing things better, faster and cheaper, few appear to be actually delivering excellence (Terrill & Middlebrooks, 2000). Too many companies strive for 'OK' but by definition 'OK' reflects the minimum acceptable level (Self, 1997). Many quality problems arise because the service proposition is producer-driven not customer-driven (Chekitan & Schultz, 2005). Globally the hotel sector is experiencing a decline in service quality but this decline appears severe because the sector had created a 'wow' effect in the 1990s (Pizam, 2004). In other words the sector had 'ratcheted up' customers' expectations to a level which they could not sustain or exceed contemporaneously. Pizam signals that hotels have deliberately lowered quality objectives and reduced performance standards to recover costs following the depression of 2001–2002. Caterer- Search.com (2002), reporting on the Which Hotel Guide for 2003, suggests that dirty rooms, petty rules and hostility towards children are just some of the problems UK hotels need to address to win back visitors. This review suggests that, service quality is an elusive concept; customers know when they receive it and when they do not. Additionally emotions, negative and positive, are increasingly important in forming service quality perceptions. However, definitions, determinants and robust delivery of service quality remain elusive. The combination of characteristics and complexity identified in the proceeding discussion leads to four propositions that become the focus of the study.

Examining customer satisfaction has been a common practice among Hospitality and Tourism researchers over the years. The main reason for continued interest in this area of research is the ever changing Hospitality business environment across the world.

The concept of Service quality has aroused considerable debate in the research literature because of the difficulties in both defining it and measuring it with no overall consensus emerging on either (Wisniewski, 2001). There are a number of different "definitions" for the meaning of service quality. Definitions of service quality by researchers have revolved around the concept that it is the result of the comparison of customers' expectations about a service and their perceptions of the way the service has been performed (Grönroos 1984; Lewis et al., 1983; Parasuraman et al.,1985; 1988).

The most common definition of service quality is 'the extent to which a service meets customers' needs or expectations' (Lewis et al.,1990; Dotchin and Oakland, 1994a;

Asubonteng et al ., 1996; Wisniewski et al., 1996). Hence Service quality is defined as the difference between customer expectations of service and perceived service. If expectations are greater than performance, then perceived quality is less than satisfactory and hence customer dissatisfaction occurs (Parasuraman et al.,1985; Lewis et al., 1990). Service quality is important to marketers because a customer's Service quality as perceived by the customer, important to both managers and researchers evaluation of service quality and the resulting level of satisfaction determine the likelihood of repurchase and ultimately affect bottomline measures of business success (Iacobucci et al., 1994)

Understanding the relationship between employee satisfaction, service quality and customer satisfaction has been focus of many empirical studies. The relationship is described as the 'satisfaction mirror' reinforcing the idea that business success results from employee satisfaction being 'reflected' in terms of customer satisfaction (Schlesinger et al., 1991; Norman et al.,1993; Liedtka et al, 1997). Silvestro et al., 2000) cast some doubts on the strength of the relationship, the balance of evidence suggests that employee satisfaction is a key driver of service quality. Voss et al (2004), for example, find that 'employee satisfaction directly affects both service quality and customer satisfaction' and Vilares et al., (2003) are so convinced about the fit that they recommend changes to one of the existing customer satisfaction indexes (ECSI) to recognise the 'cause and effect relationship between employee behaviour and customer satisfaction'.

The measurement of Service Quality has always been an important research area because of its apparent affect on cost (Crosby 1979), profitability (Buzzell et al.,1987; Rust et al., Zahorik 1993), customer satisfaction (Bolton et al.,1991), and customer retention (Reichheld et al.,1990). Service qualify indeed is regarded as a driver of corporate marketing and financial performance (Buttle 1996).

Individual firms have discovered that increasing levels of customer satisfaction can be linked to customer loyalty and profits (Heskettet al.,1997), which indicates a relationship between customer satisfaction and customer loyalty. This relationship is particularly strong when customers are very satisfied, as the research showed in the Xerox experience (Menezenes et al.,1991). Also, Enterprise Rent-A-Car learned through its research that customers who gave the highest rating to their rental experience were three times more likely to rent again than were those who gave the company the second-highest rating (Reichheld 2003).

These findings indicate clear linkages have been drawn between customer satisfaction, loyalty, and firm profitability (Zeithaml et al., 2006). Measurement of service quality allows for comparison before and after changes, for the location of quality related problems and for the establishment of clear standards for service delivery. Edvardsen et al. (1994), state that, the starting point in developing quality in services is its analysis and measurement. Measurement of service quality is vital in order to identify the areas which need improvement. It also helps to assess how much improvement is needed and evaluating the impact of the improvements once introduced. The intrinsic nature of the services namely heterogeneity, inseperability, perishability and intangibility makes the measurement of service quality a daunting task.

The impact of service quality improvements on profit, ROQ (Return on Quality) and other financial outcomes is well documented (Rust et al., 1995; Chang et al.,1998; Zeithaml, 2000; Olorunniwo et al.,2006; Gronholdt et. al., 2000). Johnson et al.,1997) emphasise the importance of understanding customer expectations as a first step in improving service quality.

In the early 1980s researchers recognized a customer's evaluation of service quality et al., Booms, 1983). Following this conceptualisation, Gronroos (1982, 1984) conceptualized service quality in terms of two dimensions: functional quality and technical quality (see Figure 2, Panel A). Gronroos (1982, 1984) defined functional quality (subjective in nature) as customers' perceptions of interactions during the service delivery process, that represented the delivery process, and the technical quality (objective in nature) that was the actual outcome that customers' received. Hence, the functional quality conceptualizes how service is offered, and the technical quality conceptualizes what is offered (Caceres et al.,2005).

Moreover, Gronroos's (1984) model measured service quality by comparing the perceived service with the expected service (Gronroos 1982, 1984; Caceres etal., 2005). Gronroos' two dimensional model that views service quality as functional and technical quality is referred to as "Nordic" perspective in the literature (Brady et al., 2001).

SERVQUAL as a multi-item scale gap model was developed by Parasuraman et al. (1985; 1988) which conceptualizes and measures elements of service that are evaluated by customers in assessing service qualify. The SERVQUAL concept lays down five dimensions to assess service quality, which are tangibles, reliability, responsiveness, assurance, and empathy with a total of 22 scale items. Parasuraman et al.'s (1985; 1988) basic model was that consumer perceptions of quality emerge from the gap between performance and expectations, as performance exceeds expectations, quality increases; and as performance decreases relative to expectations, quality decreases (Parasuraman et al., 1985; 1988). Parasuraman et al. (1988) suggested that the SERVQUAL instrument was applicable for a wide range of service and retail firms to assess customers' expectations and perceptions of service quality. In the marketing literature, the measurement of service quality from a functional point of view (eg, Parasuraman et al. 1985, 1988), is usually referred to as an "American" perspective.

SERVQUAL has been adapted to measure service quality in a variety of settings. Health care applications are numerous (Babakus et al., 1992; Bebko et al., 1995; Bowers et al., 1994; Clow et al., 1995; Headley and Miller, 1993; Licata et al., 1995; Lytle et al., 1992; O'Connor et al., 1994; Reidenbach et al.,, 1990; Woodside et al., 1989). Other settings include a dental school patient clinic, a business school placement center, a tire store, and acute care hospital (Carman, 1990); independent dental offices (McAlexander et al., 1994); at AIDS service agencies (Fusilier and Simpson, 1995); with physicians (Brown et al.,1989; Walbridge et al., 1993); in large retail chains (such as kMart, WalMart, and Target) (Teas, 1993); and banking, pest control, dry cleaning, and fast-food restaurants (Cronin and Taylor, 1992).

The majority of the work to date has attempted to use the SERVQUAL (Parasuraman et al. , 1985; 1988) methodology in an effort to measure service quality (e.g. Brooks et al., 1999; Chaston, 1994; Edvardsson et al. , 1997; Lings and Brooks, 1998; Reynoso et al., 1995; Sahney et al. , 2004; Mohammad Mehdi Mozorgi, 2006; Yunkyong Kim, 2007).

Though SERVQUAL model has been applied extensively, there has been extensive debate on the SERVQUAL methodology (Williams, 1998). Cronin et al., (1992) highlighted the conceptual and operational issues associated with the SERVQUAL scale, especially the expectation-perception gap scores. Drawing from extensive prior research on SERVQUAL and service quality, Buttle (1996) criticizes SERVQUAL's drawbacks on two aspects:

First, SERVQUAL focused on the service delivery process (functional quality which is subjective in nature) but does not emphasize the outcome of service (technical quality which is objective in nature), and the service environment when a service is rendered.

Second, SERVQUAL's dimensions are not universal and they may change across different industries (Buttle, 1996). Coulthard (2004) also reviews and critiques SERVQUAL in regard to its conceptual, methodological, and interpretative problems, and concludes further developments in new approaches are required to measure service quality.

Although, SERVQUAL has had a significant influence on academic and business communities the scale has been challenged by a number of subsequent empirical studies dealing with service qualify (Babakus and Boiler 1992; Carmen 1990; Gagliano and Hathcote 1994; Lee 2005).

SERVQUAL has led researchers to over emphasize the functional or soft aspects of service quality at the expense of the technical or hard issues (Woodall 2001). Keaveney's (1995) study found that core service failures were the biggest cause of service switching. 'A zero defects philosophy to deliver technically correct services every time should be effective in reducing customer defections.'

Process management seems to play an important role in Service Quality (Roth et al., 1995). Business process management has a significant impact on service quality. 'Business process capabilities had a larger impact on service quality than did people capabilities' and conclude that 'the area of robust business process capabilities requires greater scrutiny in service management'.

The study by Frances et al. (1997), estimates the process variation and reveals large variation in processes, reflecting large variation in firm strategy and process design. The data is from the Wharton Financial Institution Center Retail Banking study of fifty-seven of the largest bank holding companies (BHC) in the United States. This study provides support for the hypothesis that firms should systematically invest in process improvement and organizational capabilities that decrease process variation across a 'basket of processes' rather than investing in improvements that make a firm 'best of the breed' for a single process.

Ravichandran et al., (2010) revealed a high degree of concordance between the various items of servqual items which in turn speaks of service quality delivery. Banks may attempt to reposition itself by restructuring its service delivery system to enhance the Servqual items in the areas of service quality.

Service Quality in the Hotel Industry

SERVQUAL models have been used for many studies of the hospitality industry. Lehtinen and Lehtinen (1991) adopt two approaches to the analysis of service quality and its dimensions. They conducted two empirical studies in restaurants and found suitable quality dimensions for restaurant service analysis. Saleh and Ryan (1991) identify the gap between customers' perceptions of service attributes of a hotel and management perceptions of attributes of a hotel and the gap between customers' expectation of the service and perceived service quality. They argue these gaps will be a source of customers' dissatisfaction.

Johns (1992 a, b) identified gaps in the present knowledge and proposes some ideas for future research. He suggests three review articles. He defines quality and dimensions of quality in the first part and mentions sub quality and quality attributes. He adapts Khan (1982)'s study to identify factors which affect food habits and preferences and adapts Nightingale's (1985) study to identify the quality in the hotel industry. In the second part, he suggests approaches to quality management. It contributes to transfer quality management application from the manufacturing sector to hospitality industry focusing on the development of system and techniques in the hospitality industry. The third part identifies trends in the measurement and management of quality in the hospitality industry.

Saunders and Renaghan (1992) studied Total Quality Management (TQM) and differences between the manufacturing and service environments. This study highlights the potential difficulties of implementing TQM in the hospitality industry. This uses a case study of the guest service process at the Sheraton Brisbane Hotel and Towers. Sweeney, Johnson and Armstrong (1992) studied cues used by customers in product assessment and selection. They conducted an empirical study in restaurants. This study suggests which cues are most important to customers and assesses both the expected level of service and the choice of a service. They also show how these cues are traded off against each other. Specifically, Sweeney, Johnson and Armstrong (1992) test whether the cues are used differently between the expected level of service and choice of a service. Their empirical study used a student sample and different types of restaurants in different locations.

Dube, Renaghan and Miller (1994) tested restaurant service quality with a series of scenarios. They used five dimensions to measure customer satisfaction with food service. They found relative importance of service attribute in repeat-purchase intention and tradeoff process.

Stevens, Knutson and Patton (1995) adapt SERVQUAL to the restaurant industry and named it "DINESERV". The instrument consists of 40 statements that apply to restaurants. They tested internal consistency, parallelism and coefficient alpha and used confirmatory factor analysis to use DINESERV to measure restaurant dimensions. Stevens, Knutson and Patton (1995) use DINESERV to determine how customers perceive the quality of restaurant service and called it "DINESERV.per." It is designed to continually assess customers' perceptions of restaurant using a 21point interview.

DINESERV helps DINESERV.per's users determine whether a change in perceptions comes from a change of standard expectation or from a change in service quality.

Lee and Hing (1995) use SERVQUAL to measure and compare service quality in fine restaurants. This study shows that customers' expectation of service quality is higher than their perception of service quality. Assurance and reliability are the two most important dimensions of service quality in the restaurant business. Khan (1996, 2003) also adopts SERVQUAL scale to test service quality expectations of ecotourists. They adapt and revise the original SERVQUAL (Parasuraman et al., 1988) for their study and call it ECOSERV. They divide tangible factors into tangibles and eco-tangibles. Eco-tangibles ranked first with ecotourists and were followed by assurance, reliability, responsiveness, empathy, and tangibles.

Motwani, J., Kumar, A. & Youssef, M. A. (1996) examine the implementation of quality management programs in the hospitality industry. They suggest a five-stage model: awareness and commitment, planning, programming, implementing and evaluation. This study summarizes the different approaches to implementing quality management programs by hospitality organizations such as Days Inn, Hampton Inn, Four Seasons, Hilton and Marriott,.

Cheung and Law (1998) discuss human resources and their relationships with service quality and total quality management in hotel settings. They introduce the improved service quality model (ISQM) which identifies the basic components of service quality. This model's strength is of its ability to capture information from both the customers and the employees. Ekinci and Riley (1999) describe the use of the Q-sort technique in the scale development process and take the dimensions from established models of service quality. To test Q-sort methodology, they take a sample which consists of only people who have stayed in a hotel in the last year.

Pun and Ho (2001) investigate the attributes of service quality and identify ten elements which may promote quality services. The study describes an excellent service approach and the quality of service attributes and elements. These attributes and elements contribute to the organization-wide performance for sustainable long-term profitability. They suggest that creating an excellent fundamental environment includes the development of attractive service environment and the environment guides principles of quality strategies toward the service environment for restaurant operations. Lau, Akbar and Fie (2005) use a modified version of the SERVQUAL model to access the expectations and perceptions of service quality in Malaysia's four- and five-star hotels. They examine the relationship between overall satisfaction levels and the five service quality dimensions in luxury hotels.

Most service quality studies in the hospitality industry adapted the SERVQUAL scale to measure service. These studies found that SERVQUAL is useful and effective in measuring service quality in the hospitality industry. The cases of LODGSERV, DINESERV and ECOSERV also support SERVQUAL as a measure of service quality in the hospitality industry.

SERVICE QUALITY MEASUREMENT

From customers' perspective service quality has been measured since the mid 1980's. Measuring quality by counting the number of internal and external failures was done by Garvin (1983). Internal failures are observed before a product leaves the factory and external failures are incurred after a unit has been installed. Quality is conformance to the customers' not to companies' specifications.

Parasuraman, Zeithaml and Berry (1985) developed a conceptual model that define a service quality with customers' viewpoint and suggests ten factors: tangibles, reliability, responsiveness, competence, courtesy, credibility, security, accessibility, communication and understanding the customer. Parasuraman et al. (1988) modified ten dimensions of service quality into five dimensions, including 22 items that measure customer perceptions of service quality through empirical testing. Those five dimensions are tangibles (the appearance of physical facilities, equipment, personnel, and communication materials), reliability (the ability to perform the promised service accurately and dependably), responsiveness (the willingness to help customers and to provide prompt service), assurance (the knowledge and courtesy of employees and their ability to convey trust and confidence) and empathy (the caring, individualized attention provided to the customer).

Parasuraman et al. (1991a) argued that the key to providing superior service is "understanding" and "responding" to customer expectations, in order to improve the SERVQUAL scale and to verify its applicability. They conducted 16 focus group interviews with customers in six service sectors: automobile insurance, commercial property and casualty insurance, business equipment repair, truck and tractor rental and leasing, automobile repair and hotels. They used qualitative research to explore questions and quantitative research to test the relationships within the model. As a result of their study, Parasuraman, Zeithaml and Berry (1991a) eliminated the negatively expressed items, replaced two confusing items with non-redundant alternatives, and added importance weights to the measurement process. But their study results failed to support the five factor structure of the SERVQUAL scale, and did not support the empirical usefulness of the expectation items. Therefore, they recommended measuring service quality only in terms of performance.

CHAPTER 1.3

SCOPE AND METHODOLOGY

This chapter 'Scope and Methodology' contains Research framework, clarification of relevant concepts, objectives of the study, hypotheses, sampling and tools for the data collection and analysis.

1.3.1 The Research framework

Service Quality in Star Hotels is the focus of this research. This study tries to measure the quality of service of Star Hotels in the area of hotel operation. Customer satisfaction is an important issue for all hoteliers. Research has shown that there was a strong relationship between service quality and customer satisfaction.(Khaled Al-Hashash & Abdulrasoul Hussain Bahzadi, (2008). The paper discusses implications for Hotel management.

Previous studies of the components and characteristics of intangible service (Parasuraman, Zeithaml and Berry, 1988, 1991a, b, c) form the theoretical basis for this study.

A questionnaire based on the SERVQUAL ((Parasuraman, Zeithaml and Berry, 1988; 1991) was developed. The questionnaire consisted of two sections. The First part elicited sample's personal, demographic and economic characteristics information from the respondents that was deemed necessary to achieve the objectives of the study.

The second part of the questionnaire asked respondents to rate the their relative satisfaction of 50 potential factors, on their Hotel services in operations, using a ten-point scale ranging from "very important" to "not important at all".

1.3.2 Clarification of relevant concepts

Service Quality

Service quality is defined as the difference between customers' expectations for service performance prior to the service encounter and their perceptions of the service received. This is the dependent variable in this study.

Chain Hotel

Chain hotels are defined as all hotels under the ensign of a hotel group, whatever their legal status might be (subsidiaries, franchises...). The vast majority of chain hotels have an official tourism approval.

Accommodation chains are a collection or grouping of establishments under a recognizable brand name. Some chains may own each of their accommodation properties or each property may be an independently owned and operated franchise within the chain.

Standalone Hotels

Standalone Hotels are hotels which are capable of operating independently. They are not a part of any hotel chain or franchise and are self contained

SERVQUAL

SERVQUAL is a method for measuring service quality. The method was created by Parasuraman et al. (1985), as part of research projects within the field of marketing. SERVQUAL breaks service quality down to five basic dimensions; Tangibles, Reliability, Responsiveness, Assurance, and Empathy.

Gap Model of Service Quality

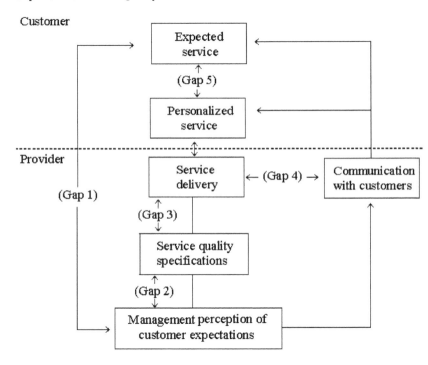

Gap 1: The difference between management perceptions of what customers expect and what customers really do expect

Gap 2: The difference between management perceptions and service quality specifications - the standards gap

Gap 3: The difference between service quality specifications and actual service delivery - are standards consistently met?

Gap 4: The difference between service delivery and what is communicated externally - are promises made consistently fulfilled?

Gap 5: The difference between what customers expect of a service and what they actually receive

Presentation

1. The presentation of the hotel is professional

2. The hotel is exclusive

3. The ambience of the hotel is relaxing

4. The hotel atmosphere is stylish

5. The hotel is first class

All the above five independent variables are related to the Hotels overall presentation aspects, and hence they are grouped together under the label Presentation variables.

Facilities of the Hotel

1. Fabulous views from the hotel room

2. Timesaving services such as valet parking

3. Floor concierge

4. Provision of gym and other recreational facilities

5. Shops within the hotel

6. High level of security

All the above six independent variables are related to the Overall Facility aspects provided by the Hotel, and hence they are grouped together under the label facilities of the Hotel variables.

Hotel Front Office

1. Check in & check out process

2. Bell desk service

3. Travel desk service

4. Billing accuracy

5. Airport service offered by the Hotel

All the above five independent variables are related to the Hotels Front office aspects that is the services provided by the front office department, and hence they are grouped together under the label Front office of the Hotel variables.

Room Product

1. Large, comfortable beds

2. Luxurious branded toiletries

3. Linen quality

4. Range of toiletries available in the bathroom

5. Provision of stationery in the room

6. Spacious room and bathrooms

7. Deluxe appliances

All the above seven independent variables are related to the Hotel Room aspects and the amenities kept in the room, and hence they are grouped together under the label Room product of the Hotel variables.

Food & Beverage Service

1. Provision of a sumptuous buffet

2. Good range of bars to buy a drink

3. Staff knowledge of menu

4. Quality of service

5. Fairly priced food and beverage

6. Economical items available for room service

7. Affordability of items in the mini bar

All the above seven independent variables are related to the Hotel Food and Beverage service aspects that is the services provided by the food and beverage service department, and hence they are grouped together under the label Food and Beverage service of the Hotel variables.

Food and Beverage production

1. Quality of food

2. Exquisite food presentation

3. Taste of food

4. Portion size of dishes

5. Provision of live counters

All the above five independent variables are related to the Hotel Food and Beverage production aspects that is the services provided by the food and beverage production department, and hence they are grouped together under the label Food and Beverage production of the Hotel variables.

Personalised Service

1. Guest relation service

2. To be acknowledged rather than to be treated as just another customer

3. To be made to feel special

4. Staff remembering your requirements

5. The staff remembers your name

All the above five independent variables are related to the Personalized service aspects that is personalized services offered to the guest by the Hotel, and hence they are grouped together under the label Personalized service of the Hotel variables.

Service In General

1. Not being kept waiting for more than a minute

2. Immediate service

3. Every need is anticipated

4. Precise attention to detail

5. Professional service

All the above five independent variables are related to the Service in general aspects provided by the hotel, and hence they are grouped together under the label service in general of the Hotel variables.

Hotel Staff

1. Staff who understand and meet unusual requests

2. High quality staff who are well trained

3. Smiling and friendly staff

4. Staff who anticipate your needs

5. Staff who understand classy patrons

All the above five independent variables are related to the Hotel staff aspects that is the quality and competency of Hotel staff , and hence they are grouped together under the label Hotel staff of the Hotel variables.

1.3.3 Objectives of the study

The study on **"Customer perception of Service Quality in Hotel Industry": A case study in Bangalore** provides empirical study towards solving the challenge for the hotel management to determine the satisfaction level of their most important service quality dimensions so as to improve on them and ultimately improve on their service quality levels. This will enable the hotel owners to retain existing customers and attract new ones at a lower cost.

The study also reveals the importance of training in Hotel Industry.

Major objectives of the study are the following

1. To assess the customer perception of service quality of Star hotels in Bangalore

2. To compare the service quality as perceived by the guest between Chain Hotels and Standalone Hotels

3. To identify and compare the gaps that may exist between the customer expectations and perceptions of service quality in Chain Hotels and Standalone Hotel guests

4. To provide recommendations that would be useful to management in designing and developing standard operating procedures and training program in the hotel

Secondary objectives which may lend support the major objectives are:

- To highlight the role of 'service quality' in the Hotel Operation.

- To identify the reasons for the difference between the service quality expectations and perceptions of Hotel guests.

- To elicit the opinion of Hoteliers about service quality.

- To offer suggestions to improve the quality of Guest service in Hotels.

1.3.4 Hypotheses

Hypotheses for Testing

Hypothesis No.	Hypothesis
1.Customer expectation of Service Quality	
H1.1	There is no significant difference between service quality expectations related to Presentation of the Hotel of Chain Hotels and Standalone Hotels.
H1.2	There is no significant difference between service quality expectations related to Facilities of the Hotel of Chain Hotels and Standalone Hotels
H1.3	There is no significant difference between service quality expectation related to Hotel front office of Standalone and Chain Hotels.
H1.4	There is no significant difference between service quality expectations related to Room product of Chain Hotels and Standalone Hotels.
H1.5	There is no significant difference between service quality expectations related to Food & Beverage Service of Standalone and Chain Hotels.

H1.6	There is no significant difference between service quality expectations of Public Sector and Private Sector Banks.
H1.7	There is no significant difference between service quality expectations related to Personalised Service of Standalone and Chain Hotels.
H1.8	There is no significant difference between service quality expectations related to Service In General of Standalone and Chain Hotels.
H1.9	There is no significant difference between service quality expectations related to Hotel staff of Standalone and Chain Hotels.
H1.10	There is no significant difference between service quality expectations related to Overall service quality of Standalone and Chain Hotels.

2.Customer Perception of Service Quality

H2.1	There is no significant difference between service quality perceptions related to Presentation of the Hotel of Chain Hotels and Standalone Hotels.
H2.2	There is no significant difference between service quality perceptions related to Facilities of the Hotel of Standalone and Chain Hotels.
H2.3	There is no significant difference between service quality perceptions related to Hotel front office of Standalone and Chain Hotels.
H2.4	There is no significant difference between service quality perceptions related to Room Product of Standalone and Chain Hotels.
H2.5	There is no significant difference between service quality perceptions related to Food & Beverage Service of Standalone and Chain Hotels.

H2.6	There is no significant difference between service quality perceptions related to Food & Beverage Product of Standalone and Chain Hotels.
H2.7	There is no significant difference between service quality perceptions related to Personalised Service of Standalone and Chain Hotels.
H2.8	There is no significant difference between service quality perceptions related to Service In General of Standalone and Chain Hotels
H2.9	There is no significant difference between service quality perceptions related to Hotel staff of Standalone and Chain Hotels.
H2.10	There is no significant difference between service quality perceptions related to Overall service quality of Standalone and Chain Hotels.
3.Gap between Customers Expected and Perceived Service Quality	
H3.1	There is no significant difference in service quality gaps (Customer Expected - Customer Perceived) relating to Presentation of Chain Hotels and Standalone Hotels.
H3.2	There is no significant difference in service quality gaps (Customer Expected - Customer Perceived) relating to Facilities of the Hotel of Chain Hotels and Standalone Hotels.
H3.3	There is no significant difference in service quality gaps (Customer Expected - Customer Perceived) relating to Hotel Front Office of Chain Hotels and Standalone Hotels.
H3.4	There is no significant difference in service quality gaps (Customer Expected - Customer Perceived) relating to Room Product of Chain Hotels and Standalone Hotels.
H3.5	There is no significant difference in service quality gaps (Customer Expected - Customer Perceived) relating to Food and Beverage Service of Chain Hotels and Standalone Hotels.
H3.6	There is no significant difference in service quality gaps (Customer

	Expected - Customer Perceived) relating to Food and Beverage Product of Chain Hotels and Standalone Hotels.
H3.7	There is no significant difference in service quality gaps (Customer Expected - Customer Perceived) relating to Personalized Service of Chain Hotels and Standalone Hotels.
H3.8	There is no significant difference in service quality gaps (Customer Expected - Customer Perceived) relating to Service in General of Chain Hotels and Standalone Hotels.
H3.9	There is no significant difference in service quality gaps (Customer Expected - Customer Perceived) relating to Hotel Staff of Chain Hotels and Standalone Hotels.
H3.10	There is no significant difference in service quality gaps (Customer Expected - Customer Perceived) relating to Overall Service Quality of Chain Hotels and Standalone Hotels.

3.6. Sampling procedure

This study is analytical in nature and is based completely on primary data collected through a scientifically structured questionnaire. The primary data were collected from the Guests of four star Hotels in Bangalore. Savannah Sarovar, Radha Hometel, Solitaire, Atria and Clarion. A quantitative approach to the study has been adopted for the study.

The primary data has been collected by survey method for gathering descriptive information by use of formal lists of questions asked to all respondents in the same way. The direct approach has been used where the researcher has asked direct questions about the services offered by the hotel e.g. "The staff remembers your name". Contact method used is through questionnaires directly given to the guests.

The study is on guests, who have experienced the services given by star hotels in Bangalore.

The researcher has selected 5 Hotels in Bangalore viz., Atria Hotel, Solitaire Hotel, Clarion Hotel, Savanah Sarovar Hotel and Radha Hometel. The researcher has chosen three standalone hotels namely Atria Hotel, Solitaire Hotel, Clarion Hotel due to the following reasons:

1. Atria Hotel, Solitaire Hotel, Clarion Hotel are well known standalone hotels in Bangalore and are sustaining themselves for more than four years in the Bangalore market.

2. Among the Standalone hotels in Bangalore these three hotels are serving to similar clientele that is business people.

Two Hotels namely Savanah Sarovar Hotel and Radha Hometel were chosen from the chain hotel category. These two Hotels have been chosen by the researcher due to the following reasons:

1. Savanah Sarovar Hotel and Radha Hometel are well known chain Hotels in Bangalore and are sustaining themselves for more than four years in the Bangalore market.

2. Among the Chain hotels in Bangalore these two hotels are serving to similar clientele that is business people.

Views of sample Hotel customers constitute primary data for the study.

1.3.6. Data Collection

The simple random sampling technique was adopted and 500 respondents, 100 from each Hotel, constitute the sample for the survey. The questionnaire was randomly distributed to all the guests staying in the star hotels selected for study.

1.3.7. Questionnaire

The primary data was collected through a structured questionnaire which was administered to the guests of Hotels to elicit their responses. The questionnaire was developed in the lines of SERVQUAL questionnaire developed by Parsuraman et. al. consisting of 9 statements relating to services offered by hotels. The list of service attributes based on different service dimensions are ranked and rated by the Guest to describe the services offered by the Hotel. The customer rated every statement on a scale of 1 to 10 where 10 being "excellent" and 1 being "worst". All the data were collected from Hotel Guest through personal contact approach.

Components of the questionnaire

Questionnaire was the only research instrument used for the study. The questionnaire had two sections; the first part captured the information on the background of the respondents: age, income level, banker and type of credit facility availed.

The second part contained 50 statements dwelling on the SERQUAL five dimensions of tangibility, empathy, accessibility, responsiveness and reliability. There were 50 statements administered keeping in mind the broad parameters. The data regarding expectations and perceptions of customers were collected in a ten point Scale. A ten-point scale can increase the variation and reliability of the responses (Nunnally, 1978). It was easy to understand (Malhotra, 1996), so the response rate was good.

Credibility of Research Findings

The credibility of the research findings was established through reliability and validity tests. Reliability means that two or more researchers, studying the same phenomenon with similar purposes, should reach approximately the same results (Gummesson, 2000). This required a standarised modus operandi through the study to ensures that in future the same study if undertaken following the same modus operandi will reach the same findings and conclusions (Yin, 2003b). Cronbach's (alpha), coefficient of reliability was used to measure the internal consistency or reliability of the data.

Validity is the extent to which a question or a scale measures what it claims to measure. Validity is divided into two main parts: a) internal validity b) external validity. Face validity can be tested is by giving the questionnaire to a sample of respondents to gauge their reaction to the items (Cavana et al., 2001).

According to Burns and Bush (1998), Content validity is a judgmental evaluation of how well the content of a scale represents the measures. The Questionnaire was validated by literature review and a pilot study.

1.3.8. Data analysis

The data collected from the respondents have been analysed by appropriate statistical techniques. Tables, diagrams and statistical results have been derived with the help of the computer software called SPSS (Statistical Package for Social Sciences).The statistical techniques used for analysis were comparison of means and "t" test.

1.3.9. Limitations of the Study

The variables taken for this study are not exhaustive. The dispositional (personality) factors were excluded. Further limitations have been included in the conclusion chapter

1.3.10. Chapterisation of the thesis

The thesis is organised in eight chapters. Chapter one **'Introduction'** introduces the study. It is divided in two sub-sections. 1(A) –Introduction to the study and 1(B) – Tourism in India Statistics. The first section talks about the relevance and reason of the study. It gives the overview of the problem and also Hospitality Industry. The chapter gives an insight on the research context. It also gives the **aim and scope of the study.** The chapter also gives **Justification and Contributions** of the Research. The second section of the introduction chapter gives support to the statistical relevance of the study by giving statistical relevance on Tourism Industry – Global Perspective, World tourism traffic, International tourism receipts, tourism in India, Economic impact of tourism in India, Important highlight of Indian tourism industry, latest tourism statistics which justify the study.

The second chapter is **Review of Literature** presents a critical appraisal of the previous work published in the literature pertaining to the topic of the investigation. The literature here is being discussed within four broad sections. The first section contains **hotel industry** specific literature relating to the characteristics of the industry, its structure and competitive forces. The second continues with the criterion **Service**. The third section relates to **service quality**, whilst the final section relates to **service quality measurement**. This structure allows comparison of research in a broader context with that in the narrower hospitality field allowing a clearer identification of the gaps in the literature that contribute to the research questions.

The third chapter is **Research and design** which compromises Research framework, clarification of relevant concepts, objectives of the study, hypotheses, sampling and tools for the data collection and analysis. In the third chapter, the research model is proposed. This chapter draws from chapter two, both in respect of identified gaps in the literature that this research will address, and in respect of insights that can be gained from the literature to support the research question and the hypotheses proposed. The chapter includes a number of hypotheses that are proposed in relation to service quality, customer satisfaction, the role of the brand in customer perceptions and loyalty intentions. The chapter finishes with an evaluation of the contribution to both theory and hotel management that will result from this research.

The forth chapter includes **Report on the present investigation/ Presentation of Findings** that is it deals with the analysis of data. The fourth chapter contains the methodological approaches utilised. The chapter commences with a section on the research design before progressing to discuss the approaches used in analysing the qualitative data gathered from the focus groups. The chapter then continues by addressing the scale development process before providing a description of the scales that resulted. The chapter continues with an explanation of the statistical methods used to analyse the data. In analysing the data, principal component analysis, regression analysis and structural equation modeling are utilised

The fifth chapter deals with **summary and Conclusions.** The results of the research are provided in the fifth chapter. The chapter commences with the qualitative research results. Following this, the demographic information relating to the sample, including sex, age, and income is presented. The chapter then continues with the exploratory factor analysis of the dimensions of hotel performance before providing confirmatory factor analyses of the dimensions of the structural model. The chapter then presents the research results for the individual hypotheses identified in Chapter 3. The fifth and final chapter contains a discussion of the results related to the overall research question, and the research hypotheses. The chapter addresses the impact of the results both from a theoretical development perspective and from that of the contribution to management in the hotel industry. This chapter also identifies limitations of this research and makes suggestions for future research.

The sixth chapter includes **Appendix.**

The seventh chapter compromises of **Literature Cited (References/ Bibliography), Publications by the candidate**

And the eighth chapter contains **Acknowledgements**

CHAPTER 1.4

REPORT ON THE PRESENT INVESTIGATION/ PRESENTATION OF
FINDINGS

ANALYSIS AND INTERPRETATION

INTRODUCTION

This chapter contains an analysis of all the hotels' assessment scores, customers' survey
and collected lagging performance figures. First, the chapter depicts the results of
SERVQUAL questionnaire administration, including a demographic profile of
participants, and the verification of the validity and reliability of the research
instrument. Then the data collected are analysed using the SPSS package, along with
standard statistical analysis techniques: Factor analysis and comparison of independent
means using t test. The following sections describe the results of each analysis in detail,
and the final result is presented. Finally, the research hypotheses are tested.

1.4.1 SERVQUAL Questionnaire Analysis

The questionnaire consisted of three parts. The first part consisted of the respondent's
profile. The second measured the respondents' expectations when dealing with an
excellent hotel. Finally, the third part measures the respondents' perceptions about the
SQ of their hotel.

A total of five hundred questionnaires were equally distributed, 100 for each hotel's
customers, through a systematic sampling method to ensure that only participating
hotels' customers were reached and all questionnaires were duly returned filled.

Data from the two parts of the questionnaires (Part A: Customer's Expectation, and B:
Customer's perception) were entered into the Statistical Package for the Social Science,
SPSS version17.0, and MS- Excel 2007 for analysis purposes. The following section

will present respondents' demographic information, in terms of age, annual income and type of credit facility availed.

PROFILES OF THE HOTELS TAKEN FOR STUDY

1. SAVANNAH SAROVAR PREMIERE

Address: #43/3 Whitefield Main Road,
Bangalore-560067

Located in Whitefield, Bangalore redefines the art of mixing business with pleasure. A five star hotel with a 104 plush rooms and a host of delightful food and beverage outlets, an open air terraced swimming pool, fitness center and all luxurious facilities that offer the discerning traveler a memorable and pleasant stay.

The hotel is located close to the globally renowned International Tech Park (ITPL) and is within close proximity to all renowned international corporate houses. Savannah Sarovar Premiere has now become the first choice hotel for most preferred business houses for their guest stay in Whitefield, Bangalore.

The attempt is to provide Comfort combined with subtle luxury for corporate travelers who prefer to stay within the reach of their Offices. Savannah Sarovar Premiere is a classic stop-over for all business travelers who come to IT hub for business. Completed with all modern facilities at an extremely affordable price, the hotel has become extremely popular among business travelers.

Facilities & Services

- ▶ Internet Access – High Speed Wi Fi / Wired Internet Access Available With Technical Support
- ▶ Business Centre Services Includes Scanning, Browsing, Secretarial Services, Video Conferencing, Teleconference Facilities
- ▶ Allamanda Pool – Outdoor Swimming Pool
- ▶ Fitness Centre
- ▶ Yoga
- ▶ Outdoor Catering
- ▶ Concierge Services Includes Tours & Travels, Flower Arrangements
- ▶ Travel Desk
- ▶ Foreign Currency Exchange
- ▶ DVD Library, Books
- ▶ Valet Parking
- ▶ Baby Sitting
- ▶ Doctor On Call
- ▶ Courier / Postal Services
- ▶ 24 Hours In Room Dining

In Room Facilities:

- ▶ Fax Machine
- ▶ Bath Tub
- ▶ Separate Bath and Shower Stall
- ▶ DVD Player
- ▶ Free Newspaper
- ▶ 24-Hour In-Room Dining
- ▶ Satellite Channels
- ▶ Non-Smoking Room
- ▶ Wake-Up Service

- ▶ Smoke Detectors In Room
- ▶ Air-Conditioned Room
- ▶ Connecting Rooms Available
- ▶ Sprinklers In Room
- ▶ Turndown Service
- ▶ 26 Inch LCD TV
- ▶ International Direct Dialing
- ▶ Down Feather Pillows
- ▶ Dual-Line Telephone

2. THE ATRIA HOTEL

Address: P.B. # 5089, # 1, Palace Road, Bangalore - 560 001

The **Atria Hotel Bangalore**, a business class hotel commenced operations in 1993. They are members of FHRAI. This business hotel in Bangalore is strategically located in the heart of the city on Palace Road. It is easily accessible to MG Road-the corporate hub of Bangalore which is just 5 kms away. It is also accessible from the airport in 45 minutes and less than 10 minutes from the city Railway station.

The Atria Hotel is known for its luxurious accommodation and comprehensive banquet facility. Dining in Bangalore is an exciting affair as the restaurants of The Atria Hotel have gained a reputation through the years and are very popular locally. This 5 star hotel is also equipped with all other facilities for both business and leisure travelers.

For your accommodations in Bangalore, Atria Hotel Bangalore offers 85 newly renovated rooms, named as lifestyle rooms, which have contemporary design and interiors to meet present day business needs and life style. A sprawling split-level atrium lobby surrounded by 168 centrally air-conditioned rooms, suites and theme suites with two scenic elevators to take bring you up to your rooms.

The Atria Hotel, a business class hotel offers high standards of hospitality on par with any international 5 star hotels at an affordable price.

The Atria Hotel Bangalore features a sprawling split-level atrium lobby surrounded by 168 centrally air-conditioned rooms, suites and theme suites. Two scenic elevators are available to take you up to your room.

85 newly renovated lifestyle rooms with contemporary design and interiors meet the needs of the present day business and leisure traveller.

With both savvy business and leisure travellers in mind, The Atria Hotel offers *great hotel services* at a *reasonable price*.

The Atria Hotel, a business class hotel, offers high standards of hospitality on par with any international 5 star hotels at an affordable price.

Facilities & Services

- ► 24 hour check-in/check-out
- ► 24 hour Front Desk
- ► 24 hour room service
- ► 24 hour House Keeping
- ► Smoking and non smoking rooms
- ► Express Check In & Check Out
- ► Luggage Storage

- ► Fitness Center
- ► Authentic & Specialty Restaurant
- ► Gift Shop
- ► Free Safe Deposit lockers
- ► Travel Desk
- ► Laundry/Dry Cleaning Service
- ► Florist
- ► Doctor on call
- ► Business Centre
- ► Foreign Exchange
- ► STD/ISD Direct Dialing
- ► Internet, Fax & Secretarial Services
- ► Wheel chair
- ► Golf arrangement on close proximity (Subject to Availability)

In Room Facilities

- ► Well Stocked Mini Bar
- ► Direct Dial Telephone
- ► Data Ports
- ► Wireless Internet Service
- ► Coffee Maker
- ► Hair Drier
- ► Magnifying shaving mirror
- ► High quality guest amenities
- ► Multi-channel entertainment
- ► Electronic Safe
- ► Daily choice of complimentary newspapers
- ► Seasonal cut fruits on request

CLARION HOTEL BENGALURU

Address: #23 Epip Zone, Whitefield, Bangalore, PIN- 560066

The Clarion Hotel Bengaluru features unique and distinctive design elements, an elegant ambiance, boutique accommodations and personalized service. This Bangalore, India hotel is conveniently located near many local businesses like Perot System, Vydehi Hospital and Eurofin.

As the capital of the state of Karnataka, Bengaluru (also known as Bangalore) boasts an abundance of notable landmarks and cultural offerings including the **Shiva statue, Bangalore Palace** and Visveswaraiah Museum. **Forum Value Shopping Mall** is nearby and has dozens of retailers and artisan shops that are perfect for finding that must-have item.

Many eateries can be found in the surrounding area. All day dining with a variety of cuisines is available in the on-site restaurant, **Va Bene**. The contemporary restaurant decorated in black and white offers buffet breakfast and lunch and an a la carte dinner. The **Atrium Lounge** provides a retro experience with 42-inch televisions and soulful music. **Le Bar** offers an array of alcoholic and non-alcoholic beverages with delectable snacks in an atmosphere primed to soothe your nerves.

Facilities & Services

As a guest of this Bangalore, India hotel, you can enjoy **amenities** like:

- ► **Free buffet breakfast**
- ► **Free weekday newspaper**
- ► **Rooftop pool**
- ► **Fitness center**
- ► **Tour desk**

This India hotel provides corporate travelers with additional conveniences including a **business center,** scanning and photocopying capabilities, **fax service,** stationery supplies and **courier service.** There are **two spacious banquet and meeting rooms** located on the premises that can accommodate up to 100 people for most functions. **Currency exchange** and **concierge services** are also available.

In Room Facilities

All elegantly appointed, spacious, **air conditioned** guest rooms are furnished with **refrigerators, coffee makers, flat-screen televisions,** wired and wireless high-speed Internet access, spacious work desks, voice mail, irons, ironing boards, robes and satellite television. Deluxe rooms and suites can be requested. Ask about rooms on **our VIP floor.**

For added convenience, **laundry facilities** are located on the premises and **free on-site basement parking** is provided. Valet parking is also available.

Whether you are traveling for business or pleasure, the Clarion Hotel Bengaluru offers an array of amenities and unique surroundings. Make a reservation with us today and enjoy our world-class, friendly and professional service.

3. RADHA HOMETEL

Address: 110C, Electronics City Phase1, Near Fire Station, Bangalore – 560100

Going with the concept of providing the best for leisure as well as business travelers, **Radha Hometel** has done well in blending the best possible amenities with the most important business facilities. Presenting a cheerful and inviting ambience, the hotel offers a world of world-class amenities. Providing the best in hospitality, the hotel presents a dedicated staff who are ever ready to make you comfortable. Conveniently located in a prime area in the city, the hotel allows easy access to its guests to all the major industrial areas and is also well-connected to other places in the city. Offering good dining and drinking options, the hotel has Flavors as their fine dining restaurant where buffets are laid for meals. At Chill, the bar, one can find a good selection of a wide range of refreshing beverages. Even when the hotel tries well to bring the best possible amenities under one roof, the aim of providing it at the best of rates is also their aim.

Rooms in Radha Hometel :

Superior Rooms: 102

Facilities & Services

- ► 24-hour front desk
- ► Air-conditioned public areas
- ► Airport transportation (surcharge)
- ► Breakfast services
- ► Business center
- ► Fitness equipment
- ► Front desk
- ► Internet access-surcharge
- ► Laundry facilities
- ► Parking (free)
- ► Room service
- ► Safe deposit box-front desk

In Room Facilities:

- ► Air-conditioning Room
- ► Cable/satellite TV
- ► Coffee/tea maker
- ► Direct-dial phone
- ► Electronic/magnetic keys
- ► Housekeeping
- ► Internet access-surcharge
- ► Internet access-wireless
- ► Mini bar/Mini Refrigerator
- ► Premium TV channels

- Refrigerator
- Television
- Wakeup-calls
- Hot and Cold running water
- Writing Desk
- Reading lamps
- Temperature Control
- Attached Bathroom
- 23 inch LCD Televisions.
- 8 inch pocket spring mattresses

4. THE SOLITAIRE HOTEL

Address: No:3, Kumarakrupa Road, Madhavnagar, Bangalore- 560001

With a prime location in the heart of the city, next to the Race Course, The Solitaire is a full facility 4 star deluxe hotel, for the discerning business traveller. Designed and built with no compromise on quality, the uniquely designed 99 rooms & suites, are complemented by gourmet restaurants, a lounge bar, and a coffee shop with an exclusive and exciting menu.

The Solitaire hotel is a premier **four star Hotel in Bangalore**. The Solitaire is located at a prime location in the heart of the city, next to the Race Course. The Solitaire is a full facility **4 star deluxe hotel in Bangalore** for the discerning business traveler. Designed and built with no compromise on quality, the uniquely designed 99 rooms & suites, are complemented by gourmet restaurants, a lounge bar, and a coffee shop with an exclusive and exciting menu. The Solitaire is equipped with the state of art facilities to cater your business needs also. We have multifunctional meetings halls and audio/video conferencing facilities. Our consistency in providing world class facilities and service has made us, one of the **best four star hotels in India**.

The Solitaire is a departure from the ordinary.

Facilities & Services

- Wi-Fi Internet Access
- LCD TV's
- Electronic Safe
- Mini Bar
- 24 Hours Room Service
- One Touch Bed Side Auto Controls

In Room Facilities:

Inside, style, service and a sense of intrigue define the experience. Guests enjoy a higher level of luxury, with unrivaled hospitality and amenities. Conceptualised based on fine gems, the name represents the rare quality that makes some precious gems stand apart. The Solitaire rooms and suites reflect these themes: Day and Night, Earth Cream, Earth Red & Neel, and they have been designed and built with exceptional quality.

The Solitaire hotel is amongst the finest Luxury Hotels in Bangalore, India. The Solitaire has 99 spacious and uniquely designed luxury rooms and suites. The exquisite decor is designed for guests to experience the best of luxury and comforts. The luxury rooms at The Solitaire contain interiors and facilities made from the finest quality materials to provide the guests with best experience. At The Solitaire, you get the amazing comforts and luxury combined with our excellent service. The names of our luxury rooms are based on fine gems. The gems represent the highest quality and our luxury rooms represent highest quality in comforts and luxury and thus The Solitaire truly stand apart.

PROFILE OF PARTICIPANTS

Respondents' distribution by Age

The next Figure 1.4.1a demonstrates participants by their age. 18% of the participants were of the age group 20 – 30 years, 46% of the participants 31 – 40 years, 24% 41 – 50 years and 12% > 51 years.

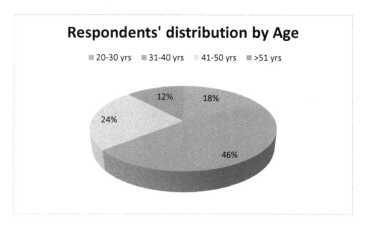

Figure 1.4.1a: Respondents' distribution by Age

Respondents' distribution by Income

The next Figure 1.4.1b demonstrates participants by their annual income. 16% of respondents had an income less than Rs. 4 lakhs per annum. 53% of the participants had an income between Rs. 4 lakhs to Rs. 6 lakhs. 31% of the participants had an income of more than Rs. 6 lakhs per annum.

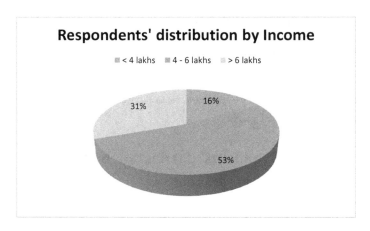

Figure 1.4.1b: Respondents' distribution by Income

Respondents' distribution by purpose of visit to the Hotels

The next Figure 1.4.1c demonstrates participants by the purpose of visit to the Hotel. 76% of the participants had visited the Hotel for Business purpose and the rest 24% visited for leisure purpose.

Figure 1.4.1c: Respondents' distribution by purpose of visit to the Hotels

1.4.2 SERVQUAL Reliability

Reliability is the ability of instruments to demonstrate overall consistency as well as internal consistency among items within each of the five service quality dimensions. The alpha coefficient is a measure for assessing the internal consistency of each dimension.

The reliability of all five dimensions was examined for each item individually (total of 22 items) using reliability test program of SPSS. Findings on table **2** revealed that the used instruments formed a cohesive scale; the test findings are demonstrated.

Cronbach'sAlpha	
Presentation	0.874
Overall Hotel	0.755
Hotel Front Office	0.849
Room Product	0.929
Food & Beverage service	0.921
Food & Beverage Product	0.936
Personalised Service	0.961
Service In General	0.875
Hotel Staff	0.832

The Cronbach's alpha reliability coefficients for the five SERVQUAL dimensions are similar across previous studies (e. g. Carman, 1990; Finn and Lamb, 1991; Babakus and Boller, 1992; Babakus and Mangold, 1992; Headley and Miller, 1993; Taylor and Baker, 1994). The lowest reliability is 0.59 reported by Finn and Lamb (1991) and the highest reliability is 0.97 reported by Babakus and Mangold (1992).

The reliability coefficient for each of the five dimensions ranged from 0.755 to 0.961. Personalised Service scored the highest alpha (0.961), followed by Room Product (0.929), Food & Beverage Product (0.921), Service In General (0.875), Presentation (0.874) and Overall Appearance of the Hotel (0.755). The overall reliability coefficient was 0.832. Thus, the gathered data are consider to be reliable, since its reported coefficient figures fall within the range of 0.93 to 0.53 that has been reported in the service quality literature. Moreover, all items received very high alpha scores, ranging from 0.668 to 0.932, and were well above the generally accepted lower limit of 0.7 (Hair et al., 1995).

1.4.3 Questionnaire Validity

The following two subsections illustrate how the used SERVQUAL questionnaire was proven to be a valid instrument, using three different methods: face and content validity, and construct (convergent) validity.

1.4.3.1 Face and content validity

Face validity is the mere appearance that a measure is valid (Kaplan and Sacuzzo, 2005). Face validity is a subjective criterion which reflects the extent to which scale items are meaningful and appear to represent the construct being measured (Parasuraman et al. 1991). Content validity is the degree to which the instrument provides an adequate representation of the conceptual domain that it is designed to cover. Apart from face validity, content validity is the only type of validity for which the evidence is subjective and logical rather than statistical (Kaplan and Sacuzzo, 2005). Content validity refers to the degree which an instrument covers the meaning of the concepts included in a particular research (Babbie, 1992).

The content validity of the proposed instrument was considered to be adequate, because the instrument had been carefully constructed, validated and refined by PZB supported by an extensive literature review. The questionnaire was then passed by the researcher to specialists in this area, who were requested to review the questionnaire and determine the suitability and difficulty of the questions. The final questionnaire version then followed their comments and suggestions. Additionally, considering the advice of Nunnally (1978) that any pre-test must be carried out on a similar group, the researcher completed a pilot study by distributing the questionnaire to a similar target audience. 25 people were asked if the completion of the questionnaire created any difficulties. All respondents replied that they faced no problems in completing the questionnaires. Hence the instrument can be considered to have face and content validity.

1.4.3.2 Factor rotation and factor loading

KMO Kaiser-Meyer-Olkin (KMO) and Bartlett's test was done to measure the sampling adequacy which should be greater than 0.5 to do a satisfactory factor analysis. The KMO measure is 0.880. From the same table, we can see that the Bartlett's test of sphericity is significant. That is, its associated probability is less than 0.05. This means that the correlation matrix is not an identity matrix.

KMO and Bartlett's Test			
Kaiser-Meyer-Olkin Measure of Sampling Adequacy.			.880
Bartlett's Test of Sphericity		Approx. Chi-Square	26733.455
		df	1225
		Sig.	.000

On being satisfied with the five chosen dimensions, the loading of all the items within the five dimensions was examined. The Varimax technique for rotated component analysis was used with a cut-off point for interpretation of the factors at 0.40 or greater. The results are summarised in Table on the next page.

Rotated Component Matrix[a]										
	Component									
	1	2	3	4	5	6	7	8	9	10
Professional service	.790									
Every need is anticipated	.751									
High quality staff who are well trained	.744									
Smiling and friendly staff	.700									
Staff who understand and meet unusual requests	.680									
Precise attention to detail	.675									
Not being kept waiting for more than a minute	.652									
Immediate service	.645									
Billing accuracy	.559									
Provision of live counters	.543									

Check in & check out process	.486									
Staff who understand classy patrons	.467									
Spacious room and bathrooms		.833								
Deluxe appliances		.828								
Provision of stationery in the room		.819								
Luxurious branded toiletries		.740								
Large, comfortable beds		.712								
Linen quality		.636								
Range of toiletries available in the bathroom		.569								
Staff knowledge of menu		.451								
Staff remembering your requirements			.896							
The staff remember your name			.879							

To be made to feel special		.864								
Guest relation service		.862								
To be acknowledged rather than to be treated as just another customer		.860								
Timesaving services such as valet parking			.746							
Fabulous views from the hotel room			.707							
Floor concierge			.706							
The hotel is exclusive			.695							
The presentation of the hotel is professional			.624							
The hotel atmosphere is stylish			.595							
Provision of gym and other recreational facilities			.546							
The ambience of the hotel is relaxing			.444							

The hotel is first class				.38 7					
Exquisite food presentation				.77 3					
Taste of food				.75 8					
Quality of food				.73 6					
Bell desk service				.58 0					
Portion size of dishes				.57 4					
Travel desk service				.42 7					
Economical items available for room service					.70 6				
Affordability of items in the mini bar					.70 0				
Fairly priced food and beverage					.60 2				
Quality of service					.58 6				
Good range of bars to buy a drink					.57 3				

Provision of a sumptuous buffet						.55 2				
Airport service offered by the Hotel						.58 3				
High level of security							.62 2			
Staff who anticipate your needs								.74 7		
Shops within the hotel										.79 9

All items were loaded onto the expected dimension for which they were designed. Factor loadings were all higher than 0.4 so that each item loaded higher on its associated construct than on any other construct. As suggested by Hair et al. (1998), a factor loading higher than 0.35 is considered statistically significant at an alpha level of 0.05. This supports the discriminate validity of the measurement

1.4.4 To compare Customer Expectation of Service quality between Chain Hotels and Standalone Hotels

1.4.4.1 Dimension – Presentation of the Hotel

$H_{1.1}$: There is no significant difference between service quality expectations related to Presentation of the Hotel of Chain Hotels and Standalone Hotels.

Presentation of the Hotel

Group Statistics

	Hotel	N	Mean	Std. Deviation	Std. Error Mean
Presentation	Chain	200	44.6550	6.50983	.46031
	Standalone	300	42.8167	9.02744	.52120

Independent Samples Test

		Levene's Test for Equality of Variances		t-test for Equality of Means					95% Confidence Interval of the Difference	
		F	Sig.	t	df	Sig. (2-tailed)	Mean Difference	Std. Error Difference	Lower	Upper
Presentation	Equal variances assumed	1.621	.204	2.481	498	.013	1.83833	.74085	.38275	3.29392

			2.64 4	494.92 5	.008	1.83833	.69537	.4720 9	3. 7
Equal variances not assumed									

The Mean of Chain Hotels was 44.655 and the standard deviation 6.509. The Mean of Standalone Hotels was 42.816 and the Standard Deviation 9.0274. An Independent samples t-test was conducted to examine whether there was a significant difference between service quality expectation of presentation of the Hotel between Customers of Standalone and Chain Hotels. The p-value (sig.) for the Levene's test .204), is above .05, hence equal variances are assumed. The test revealed that there is no statistically significant difference between Standalone and Chain Hotel Customers (t = 2.481, df = 498 p <.05). Hence the hypothesis that that there is no significant difference in service quality expectations of Presentation of the Hotel between Standalone and Chain Hotel Customers is accepted

1.4.4.2 Dimension – Facilities of the Hotel

$H_{1.2}$: There is no significant difference between service quality expectations related to Facilities of the Hotel of Chain Hotels and Standalone Hotels.

Facilities of the Hotel

Group Statistics

	Hotel	N	Mean	Std. Deviation	Std. Error Mean
Facilities of the Hotel	Chain	200	52.3550	8.36173	.59126
	Standalone	300	49.8633	11.35228	.65542

Independent Samples Test

		Levene's Test for Equality of Variances		t-test for Equality of Means					95% Confidence Interval of the Difference	
		F	Sig.	t	df	Sig. (2-tailed)	Mean Difference	Std. Error Difference	Lower	Upper
Facilities of the Hotel	Equal variances assumed	10.612	.001	2.660	498	.008	2.49167	.93682	.65106	4.33227
	Equal variances not assumed			2.823	493.051	.005	2.49167	.88271	.75733	4.22600

The Mean of Chain Hotels was 52.355 and the standard deviation 8.361. The Mean of Standalone Hotels was 49.863 and the Standard Deviation 11.352. An Independent samples t-test was conducted to examine whether there was a significant difference between service quality expectation of Facilities of the Hotel between Customers of Standalone and Chain Hotels. The p-value (sig.) for the Levene's test (.001), is below .05, hence equal variances are not assumed. The test revealed that there is no statistically significant difference between Standalone and Chain Hotel Customers (t = 2.823, df = 493.05 p <.05). Hence the hypothesis that that there is no significant difference in service quality expectations of Facilities of the Hotel between Standalone and Chain Hotel Customers is accepted

1.4.4.3 Dimension – Hotel front office

$H_{1.3}$: There is no significant difference between service quality expectation related to Hotel front office of Standalone and Chain Hotels.

Hotel front office

Group Statistics

	Hotel	N	Mean	Std. Deviation	Std. Error Mean
Hotel Front Office	**Chain**	200	44.9000	6.34498	.44866
	Standalone	300	43.9233	6.99623	.40393

Independent Samples Test

		Levene's Test for Equality of Variances		t-test for Equality of Means					95% Con Interval o Difference	
		F	Sig.	t	df	Sig. (2-tailed)	Mean Differ ence	Std. Error Differ ence	Lower	U
Hotel Front office	Equal variances assumed	.251	.61	1.587	498	.113	.97667	.61560	-.23282	2
	Equal variances not assumed			1.618	453.87	.106	.97667	.60370	-.20972	2

The Mean of Chain Hotels was 44.900 and the standard deviation 6.344. The Mean of Standalone Hotels was 43.923 and the Standard Deviation 6.996. An Independent samples t-test was conducted to examine whether there was a significant difference between service quality expectations of Hotel Front office between Customers of Standalone and Chain Hotels. The p-value (sig.) for the Levene's test . .617), is above .05, hence equal variances are assumed. The test revealed a statistically significant difference between Standalone and Chain Hotel Customers (t = -1.587, df = 498 p > .05). Hence the hypothesis that that there is significant difference in service quality expectations of Hotel Front office between Standalone and Chain Hotel Customers is rejected. Hotel Front office of Chain Hotels (mean = 44.900, sd = 6.344) is expected to be of higher quality than Standalone Hotels (mean = 43.923, sd = 6.996).

Mean of Individual Items under Hotel Front office

	Chain	Standalone
1. Check in & check out process	9.08	8.95
2. Bell desk service	9.12	8.94
3.Travel desk service	9.06	8.73
4. Billing accuracy	8.91	8.81
5. Airport service offered by the Hotel	8.74	8.50
Overall	8.98	8.78

If we compare the services expectation of guest from Chain Hotels as compared with Standalone hotels s much higher. In the criteria "**Check in & check out process**" Chain hotels have scored better by getting a score of 9.08 against 8.95 scored by Standalone hotels. In the "**Travel desk service**" again the Chain hotels have scored better by getting a score of 9.06 against 8.73 scored by Standalone hotels. In "**Billing accuracy**" Chain Hotels have a better score of 8.91 as against 8.81 scored by

Standalone hotels. In the **"Bell desk service"** Chain hotels have been expected to do extremely well by scoring 9.12 as against 8.94 scored by Standalone hotels

Even in the criteria **"Airport service offered by the Hotel"** Chain hotels have scored 8.74 as compared to 8.50 scored by Standalone hotels. The guest have expected that the airport services of Chain Hotels should be better than Standalone.

If we see the **"Overall"** scoring of front office services of Chain Hotels and Standalone hotels, Chain hotels have performed very well that is the guest expectation from Chain hotels are very high as compared to Standalone Hotels giving a score of 8.98 as compared to Standalone hotels with a score of 8.78

1.4.4.4 Dimension – Room product

$H_{1.4}$: There is no significant difference between service quality expectations related to Room product of Chain Hotels and Standalone Hotels.

Room product

Group Statistics

	Hotel	N	Mean	Std. Deviation	Std. Error Mean
Room product	Chain	200	61.4800	8.82548	.62406
	Standalone	300	60.4000	11.53967	.66624

Independent Samples Test

		Levene's Test for Equality of Variances		t-test for Equality of Means					95% Confidence Interval of the Difference	
		F	Sig.	t	df	Sig. (2-tailed)	Mean Difference	Std. Error Difference	Lower	Upper
Room product	Equal variances assumed	.079	.778	1.123	498	.262	1.08000	.96210	-.81027	2.970 27
	Equal variances not assumed			1.183	488.654	.237	1.08000	.91287	-.71363	2.873 63

The Mean of Chain Hotels was 61.480 and the standard deviation 8.825. The Mean of Standalone Hotels was 60.400 and the Standard Deviation 11.539. An Independent samples t-test was conducted to examine whether there was a significant difference between service quality expectation of Room product of the Hotel between Customers of Standalone and Chain Hotels. The p-value (sig.) for the Levene's test .778), is above .05, hence equal variances are assumed. The test revealed a statistically significant difference between expectation of Standalone and Chain Hotel Customers (t = 1.123, df = 498 p > .05). Hence the hypothesis that that there is significant difference in service quality expectations of Room Product between Standalone and Chain Hotel Customers is rejected. Room product of Chain Hotels (mean = 61.480, sd = 8.825) is expected to be of higher quality than Standalone Hotels (mean = 60.400, sd = 11.539).

Mean of Individual Items under Room Product

	Chain	Standalone
1. Large, comfortable beds	8.82	8.60
2. Luxurious branded toiletries	8.69	8.71
3. Linen quality	8.68	8.59
4. Range of toiletries available in the bathroom	8.61	8.54
5. Provision of stationery in the room	8.76	8.67
6. Spacious room and bathrooms	8.98	8.61
7. Deluxe appliances	8.96	8.68
Total	8.78	8.63

The expectation of guest as far as room product goes is higher from Chain Hotels than Standalone hotels. In providing **"Large, comfortable beds"** Chain hotels have scored better by getting a score of 8.82 against 8.60 scored by Standalone hotels. Also in giving **"Linen quality"** Chain hotels have scored better by getting a score of 8.68 against 8.59 scored by Standalone hotels. In providing **"Range of toiletries available in the bathroom"** Chain hotels have scored better by getting a score of 8.61 against 8.54 scored by Standalone hotels. The guest expects better range of toiletries in Chain hotels than in standalone Hotels. In providing **"Provision of stationery in the room"** Chain hotels have scored better by getting a score of 8.76 against 8.67 scored by Standalone hotels. In providing stationeries Chain hotels are expected to provide more number and better stationeries than Standalone hotels like personalized stationary with guest name written on the letter head etc. The guest expectation in providing **"Spacious room and bathrooms"** Chain hotels have scored better by getting a score of 8.96 against 8.68 scored by Standalone hotels. Large rooms and bathroom with ample amenities is what the guest expects from Chain hotels. If we see the **"Total"** Chain hotels have scored better by getting a score of 8.78 against 8.63 scored by Standalone hotels. This indicates that the guest expectation from Chain hotels is very high as far as room products are concerned. The only criteria where the Standalone hotels are expected better are in providing **"Large, comfortable beds"** where Standalone hotels have scored better by getting a score of 7.56 against 8.14 scored by Chain hotels and **"Luxurious branded toiletries"** where Standalone hotels have scored better by getting a score 8.69 against 8.71 scored by Chain hotels. Today's clientele is brand conscious and thus expects hotels to have branded amenities in the rooms.

1.4.4.5 Dimension - Food & Beverage Service

$H_{1.5}$: There is no significant difference between service quality expectations related to Food & Beverage Service of Standalone and Chain Hotels.

Food & Beverage Service
Group Statistics

	Hotel	N	Mean	Std. Deviation	Std. Error Mean
FBP Service	Chain	200	64.8850	5.68448	.40195
	Standalone	300	60.5467	12.14907	.70143

Independent Samples Test

		Levene's Test for Equality of Variances		t-test for Equality of Means					95% Conf Interval Difference	
		F	Sig.	t	Df	Sig. (2-tailed)	Mean Difference	Std. Error Difference	Lower	
FBP Service	Equal variances assumed	28.331	.000	4.716	498	.000	4.33833	.91983	2.53110	
	Equal variances not assumed			5.366	454.050	.000	4.33833	.80843	2.74960	

The Mean of Chain Hotels was 64.885 and the standard deviation 5.684. The Mean of Standalone Hotels was 60.546 and the Standard Deviation 12.149. An Independent samples t-test was conducted to examine whether there was a significant difference between service quality expectation of food and beverage Service between Customers of Standalone and Chain Hotels. The p-value (sig.) for the Levene's test (.000), is below .05, hence equal variances are not assumed. The test revealed that there is no statistically significant difference between expectation of Standalone and Chain Hotel Customers (t = 4.716, df = 493 p <.05). Hence the hypothesis that that there is no significant difference in service quality expectations of food and beverage service between Standalone and Chain Hotel Customers is accepted

1.4.4.6 Dimension- Food and Beverage production

$H_{1.6}$: There is no significant difference between service quality expectations related to Food & Beverage Product of Standalone and Chain Hotels.

Food and Beverage production

Group Statistics

	Hotel	N	Mean	Std. Deviation	Std. Error Mean
FBP Product	**Chain**	200	200	45.0600	6.95527
	Standalone	300	300	45.3067	7.02975

Independent Samples Test

								t-test for Equality of Means		
Levene's Test for Equality of Variances									95% Confidence Interval of the Difference	
		F	Sig.	t	df	Sig. (2-tailed)	Mean Differen ce	Std. Error Difference	Lower	Upper
FBP Product	**Equal variances assumed**	.708	.401	-.386	498	.700	-.24667	.63902	-1.50217	1.00884

			-	429.	.699	-.24667	.63765	-	1.(
Equal variances not assumed			.38 7	702				1.4999 8	4

The Mean of Chain Hotels was 45.060 and the standard deviation 6.955. The Mean of Standalone Hotels was 45.306 and the Standard Deviation 7.029. An Independent samples t-test was conducted to examine whether there was a significant difference between service quality expectation of Food & Beverage Product of Standalone and Chain Hotels. The p-value (sig.) for the Levene's test (.401) , is above .05, hence equal variances are assumed. The test revealed a statistically significant difference between Standalone and Chain Hotel Customers (t = -.386, df = 498 p > .05). Hence the hypothesis that that there is no significant difference in service quality expectations of food and beverage Product between Standalone and Chain Hotel Customers is rejected. Food and beverage Product of Standalone Hotels (mean = 45.306, sd = 7.029) is perceived to be of higher quality than Chain Hotels (mean = 45.060, sd = 6.955).

Mean of Individual Items under Food and Beverage Product

	Chain	Standalone
1. Quality of food	8.99	9.00
2. Exquisite food presentation	8.99	8.98
3. Taste of food	9.01	9.21
4. Portion size of dishes	8.96	9.12
5. Provision of live counters	9.12	9.00
Overall	9.01	9.06

In providing "**Quality of food**" the guest's expectation from Standalone hotels is much higher than Chain Hotels. The guests have scored Standalone hotels 9.00 as against Chain Hotels with 8.99. In the criteria "**Taste of food**" guests have scored Standalone hotels 9.21 as compared to Chain Hotels with 9.01. The guest expectation of better quality food is higher from Standalone Hotels.

In the criteria "**Portion size of dishes**" again the guest have expected Standalone Hotels to give better portion size and given a rating of 9.12 as against 8.96 scoring given to Chain Hotels

In providing "**Provision of live counters**" guest expectation from Chain hotels is higher. The guest expects more live counter in Chain hotels than in Standalone hotels. The guests have scored Chain hotels as 9.12 as compared to Standalone hotels with 9.00 scoring. Also in "**Exquisite food presentation**" the guest expectation from Chain hotels is high with a scoring of 8.99 for Chain hotels as compared as 8.98 for Standalone Hotels

If we see "**Overall**" expectation as far as food and beverage product is concerned, the expectation form Standalone hotels are much higher as compared to Chain Hotels. The guests have scored Standalone hotels with 9.06 as compared to 9.01 scored by Chain Hotels

1.4.4.7 Dimension - Personalised Service

H_{17}: There is no significant difference between service quality expectations related to Personalised Service of Standalone and Chain Hotels.

Personalised Service

Group Statistics

	Hotel	N	Mean	Std. Deviation	Std. Error Mean
Personalised service	Chain	200	45.3700	7.84335	.55461
	Stand alone	300	44.1600	10.60200	.61211

Independent Samples Test

			t-test for Equality of Means							
Levene's Test for Equality of Variances									95% Confid Interval of Difference	
		F	Sig.	t	df	Sig. (2-tailed)	Mean Differenc e	Std. Error Differen ce	Lower	Uppe
Person alised service	Equal variances assumed	7.7 47	.00 6	1.38 1	498	.168	1.21000	.87592	-.51096	2.930
	Equal variances not assumed			1.46 5	492 .60 9	.144	1.21000	.82599	-.41291	2.832

The Mean of Chain Hotels was 45.370 and the standard deviation 7.843. The Mean of Standalone Hotels was 44.160 and the Standard Deviation 10.602. An Independent samples t-test was conducted to examine whether there was a significant difference between service quality expectation of Personalised Service of Standalone and Chain Hotels. The p-value (sig.) for the Levene's test (.006) is more than .05, hence equal variances are assumed. The test revealed that statistically there is significant difference between Standalone and Chain Hotel Customers (t = -1.381 df = 498, p > .05). Hence the hypothesis that that there is no significant difference in service quality expectations of Personalised Service between Standalone and Chain Hotel Customers is rejected. . Personalised Service of Chain Hotels (mean =45.370, sd = 7.843) is expected to be of higher quality than Standalone Hotels (mean = 44.160, sd = 10.602).

Mean of Individual Items under Personalised Service

	Chain	Standalone
1. Guest relation service	9.14	9.00
2. To be acknowledged rather than to be treated as just another customer	9.05	8.85
3. To be made to feel special	8.98	8.79
4. Staff remembering your requirements	9.17	8.77
5. The staff remember your name	9.04	8.75
Overall	9.07	8.83

The expectation of guest as far as Personalised service goes is higher from Chain Hotels than Standalone hotels. In providing **"Guest relation service"** Chain hotels have scored better by getting a score of 9.14 against 9.00 scored by Standalone hotels. Also in giving **"To be acknowledged rather than to be treated as just another customer"** Chain hotels have scored better by getting a score of 9.05 against 8.85 scored by Standalone hotels. In the criteria **"To be made to feel special"** Chain hotels have scored 8.98 against 8.79 scored by Standalone hotels. And in **"Staff remembering your requirements"** again Chain hotels have scored 9.17 against 8.77 scored by

Standalone hotels. The same goes with the criteria "**The staff remember your name**" where again Chain hotels have scored 9.04 against 8.75 scored by Standalone hotels. All the above score clearly indicates that the guest expectation of personalized service from Chain hotels is extremely high. Considering the   fact that even when we see the overall score Chain hotels have scored 9.07 against 8.83 scored by Standalone hotels. The difference in the score is big and is a clear indication of the service expectation of the guests from the Hotels. The guests expects the Chain hotels to be more standardized and staff being more professional in handling guests services.

1.4.4.8 Dimension – Service In General

$H_{1.8}$: There is no significant difference between service quality expectations related to Service In General of Standalone and Chain Hotels.

Service In General

Group Statistics

		Hotel	N	Mean	Std. Deviation	Std. Mean
Service In General		Chain	200	44.9900	6.83105	.48303
		Standalone	300	44.9633	6.29503	.36344

Independent Samples Test

Levene's Test for Equality of Variances				t-test for Equality of Means					95% Confidence Interval of the Difference	
		F	Sig.	t	df	Sig. (2-tailed)	Mean Difference	Std. Error Difference	Lower	Upper
Service In General	Equal variances assumed	2.489	.115	.045	498	.964	.02667	.59469	-1.14175	1.19508
	Equal variances not assumed			.044	402.292	.965	.02667	.60449	-1.16169	1.21502

The Mean of Chain Hotels was 44.990 and the standard deviation 6.831. The Mean of Standalone Hotels was 44.963 and the Standard Deviation 6.295. An Independent samples t-test was conducted to examine whether there was a significant difference between service quality expectation of Service In General of Standalone and Chain Hotels. The p-value (sig.) for the Levene's test (.115) is more than .05, hence equal variances are assumed. The test revealed that statistically there is significant difference between Standalone and Chain Hotel Customers (t = .045 df = 498, p > .05). Hence the hypothesis that that there is no significant difference in service quality expectation of Service In General between Standalone and Chain Hotel Customers is rejected. . Service In General of the Hotel of Chain Hotels (mean =44.990, sd = 6.831) is expected to be of higher quality than Standalone Hotels (mean = 44.963, sd = 6.295).

Mean of Individual Items under Service in general

	Chain	Standalone
1. Not being kept waiting for more than a minute	9.01	8.81
2. Immediate service	9.20	9.07
3. Every need is anticipated	8.89	9.07
4. Precise attention to detail	8.78	9.02
5. Professional service	9.12	9.00
Overall	9.00	8.99

In providing "**Not being kept waiting for more than a minute**" Chain hotels have scored better by getting a score 9.01 of against 8.81 scored by Standalone hotels. Also in providing "**Immediate service**" Chain hotels have scored better by getting a score 9.20 of against 9.07 scored by Standalone hotels. In the criteria "**Professional service**" Chain hotels have scored better by getting a score 9.12 against 9.00 scored by Standalone hotels. But if we see the criteria "**Every need is anticipated**" Standalone hotels have scored better by getting a score 9.07 of against 8.89 scored by Chain hotels.

Also in providing "**Precise attention to detail**" Standalone hotels have scored better by getting a score 8.78 of against 9.02 scored by Chain hotels. "**Overall**" Chain Hotels have scored better with a scoring of 9.00 as against Standalone Hotels who have scored 8.99.

The expectation of guest about service in general from Chain Hotels as well as Standalone Hotels is similar. In few categories like Not being kept waiting for more than a minute, Immediate service and Professional service, the guest expectations from Chain hotels is higher whereas in criteria's like Every need is anticipated and Precise attention to detail, the expectations of guest from Standalone hotels is higher. But overall the guests expect better service from Chain Hotels than Standalone Hotels. The reason might be the overall impression of the guests about the Chain properties or the experience in other properties of same Chain.

1.4.4.9 Dimension – Hotel staff

$H_{1.9}$: There is no significant difference between service quality expectations related to Hotel staff of Standalone and Chain Hotels.

Hotel staff

Group Statistics

	Hotel	N	Mean	Std. Deviation	Std. Error Mean
Hotel staff	**Chain**	200	45.3600	6.60823	.46727
	Standalone	300	44.4867	6.65513	.38423

Independent Samples Test

				t-test for Equality of Means				
Levene's Test for Equality of Variances								95% Confidence Interval of the Difference
		F	Sig.	T	df	Sig. (2-tailed)	Mean Differen ce	Std. Error Differ ence	Lower
Hotel Staff	Equal varian ces assum ed	.097	.756	1.442	498	.150	.87333	.60582	-.31695
	Equal varian ces not assum ed			1.444	428.65 9	.150	.87333	.60496	-.31573

The Mean of Chain Hotels was 45.360 and the standard deviation 6.608. The Mean of Standalone Hotels was 44.486 and the Standard Deviation 6.655. An Independent samples t-test was conducted to examine whether there was a significant difference between service quality expectation of Hotel Staff of Standalone and Chain Hotels. The p-value (sig.) for the Levene's test (.756) is more than .05, hence equal variances are assumed. The test revealed that statistically there is significant difference between Standalone and Chain Hotel Customers (t = 1.442   df = 498, p > .05). Hence the hypothesis that that there is no significant difference in service quality expectation of Hotel staff between Standalone and Chain Hotel Customers is rejected. . Hotel staff of Chain Hotels (mean =45.360, sd = 6.608) is expected to be of higher quality than Standalone Hotels (mean = 44.486, sd = 6.655).

Mean of Individual Items under Hotel Staff

	Chain	Standalone
1. Staff who understand and meet unusual requests	9.15	8.95
2. High quality staff who are well trained	9.15	9.06
3. Smiling and friendly staff	9.15	8.80
4. Staff who anticipate your needs	8.88	8.79
5. Staff who understand classy patrons	9.05	8.89
Overall	9.07	8.90

In providing "**Staff who understand and meet unusual requests**" Chain hotels have scored better by getting a score of 9.15 against 8.95 scored by Standalone hotels. Also in providing "**High quality staff who are well trained**" Chain hotels have scored better by getting a score of 9.15 against 9.06 scored by Standalone hotels. In the criteria "**Smiling and friendly staff** "again Chain hotels have scored better by getting a score of 9.15 against 8.80 scored by Standalone hotels. In providing "**Staff who anticipate your needs**" Chain hotels have scored better by getting a score of 8.88 against   8.79

scored by Standalone hotels. In the criteria **"Staff who understand classy patrons"**

Chain hotels have scored better by getting a score of 9.05 against 8.89 scored by Standalone hotels. When we look at **"Overall"** scores Chain hotels have scored better by getting a score of 9.07 against 8.90 scored by Standalone hotels.

The scores clearly indicate that the expectation of Hotel staff from Chain hotels as compared to Standalone Hotels is very high. The guest expects that the staff of Chain hotels is well trained. The staff should be able to understand the guest needs. They should be friendly and polished. Rather than the guest asking for service the staff should be able to anticipate their need. The staff should be able to understand the type of guest like business or family and also the strata they come from and the staff should treat the guest with that. The expectations from the guest about the staff of Chain hotels comprise of all these qualities and are extremely high as compared to Standalone properties.

1.4.4.10 Dimension – Overall service quality

$H_{1.10}$: There is no significant difference between service quality expectations related to Overall service quality of Standalone and Chain Hotels.

Overall service quality

Group Statistics

	Hotel	N	Mean	Std. Deviation	Std. Mean
Overall service quality	Chain	200	449.0550	49.38109	3.4917
	Standalone	300	436.4667	69.36402	4.0047

Independent Samples Test

				t-test for Equality of Means						
Levene's Test for Equality of Variances									95% Confidence Interval of the Difference	
		F	Sig.	t	Df	Sig. (2-tailed)	Mean Differen ce	Std. Error Differ ence	Lower	Up per
Overall service quality	Equal variances assumed	7.309	.007	2.219	498	.027	12.58833	5.6738 9	1.44061	23. 736 06
	Equal variances not assumed			2.369	495.845	.018	12.58833	5.3132 2	2.14912	23. 027 54

The Mean of Chain Hotels was 449.055 and the standard deviation 49.381. The Mean of Standalone Hotels was 436.466 and the Standard Deviation 69.364. An Independent samples t-test was conducted to examine whether there was a significant difference between overall service quality expectation of Standalone and Chain Hotels. The p-value (sig.) for the Levene's test (.007) is more than .05, hence equal variances are assumed. The test revealed that statistically there is no significant difference between Standalone and Chain Hotel Customers (t = 2.219 df = 498, p < .05). Hence the hypothesis that that there is no significant difference in overall service quality between Standalone and Chain Hotel Customers is accepted.

1.4.5 To compare Customer Perception of Service quality between Chain Hotels and Standalone Hotels

1.4.5.1 Dimension – Presentation of the Hotel

$H_{2.1}$: There is no significant difference between service quality perceptions related to Presentation of the Hotel of Chain Hotels and Standalone Hotels.

Presentation of the Hotel

Group Statistics

	Hotel	N	Mean	Std. Deviation	Std. Error Mean
Presentation	Chain	200	38.6350	5.06954	.35847
	Standalone	300	39.9900	7.62871	.44044

Independent Samples Test

		Levene's Test for Equality of Variances		t-test for Equality of Means					95% Confide Interval of Difference	
		F	Sig.	t	df	Sig. (2-tailed)	Mean Differe nce	Std. Error Difference	Lower	Upper
Present ation	Equal variances assumed	.001	.97 3	-2.208	498	.028	-1.3550 0	.61381	-2.56098	-.1490.
	Equal variances not assumed			-2.386	497 .99 7	.017	-1.3550 0	.56788	-2.47074	-.2392

The Mean of Chain Hotels was 38.635 and the standard deviation 5.069. The Mean of Standalone Hotels was 39.990 and the Standard Deviation 5.069. An Independent samples t-test was conducted to examine whether there was a significant difference between service quality perceptions of Presentation of the Hotel between Customers of Standalone and Chain Hotels. The p-value (sig) for the Levene's test (.973), is above .05, hence equal variances are assumed. The test revealed that statistically there is no significant difference between Standalone and Chain Hotel Customers (t = -2.208, df = 498, p =.028 which is <.05). Hence the hypothesis that that there is no significant difference in service quality perceptions of Presentation of the Hotel between Standalone and Chain Hotel Customers is accepted.

1.4.5.2 Dimension Facilities of the Hotel

$H_{2.2}$: There is no significant difference between service quality perceptions related to Facilities of the Hotel of Standalone and Chain Hotels.

Facilities of the Hotel

Group Statistics

	Hotel	N	Mean	Std. Deviation	Std. Error Mean
Facilities of the Hotel	Chain	200	46.2300	6.61919	.46805
	Standalone	300	45.1167	8.70684	.50269

Independent Samples Test

		Levene's Test for Equality of Variances		t-test for Equality of Means					95% Confidence Interval of Difference	
		F	Sig.	t	df	Sig. (2-tailed)	Mean Difference	Std. Error Difference	Lower	Up
Facilities of the Hotel	Equal variances assumed	.06 6	.798	1.536	498	.125	1.11333	.72471	- .31052	2.5 9
	Equal variances not assumed			1.621	489 .44 4	.106	1.11333	.68685	- .23621	2.4 8

The Mean of Chain Hotels was 46.230 and the standard deviation 6.619. The Mean of Standalone Hotels was 45.11and the Standard Deviation 8.706. An Independent samples t-test was conducted to examine whether there was a significant difference between service quality perceptions of Facilities of the Hotel between Customers of Standalone and Chain Hotels. The p-value (sig.) for the Levene's test .798), is above .05, hence equal variances are assumed. The test revealed a statistically significant difference between Standalone and Chain Hotel Customers (t = 1.589, df = 498 p > .05). Hence the hypothesis that that there is no significant difference in service quality perceptions of Facilities of the Hotel between Standalone and Chain Hotel Customers is rejected. Facilities of Chain Hotels (mean = 46.230, sd = 6.619) is perceived to be of higher quality than Standalone Hotels (mean = 45.11, sd = 8.7068).

Mean of Individual Items under Facilities of the Hotel

	Chain	Standalone
1. Fabulous views from the hotel room	7.35	7.80
2. Timesaving services such as valet parking	7.90	7.90
3. Floor concierge	7.67	7.71
4. Provision of gym and other recreational facilities	8.03	7.90
5. Shops within the hotel	7.48	5.88
6. High level of security	7.81	7.92
Overall	9.25	9.02

When we looked into the Chain Hotels scored less than Standalone Hotels in giving **"Fabulous views from the hotel room"**, The Standalone hotel have to attract customers based on their location . Hence they give more attention to the view from the rooms. They understand the importance of retaining the customer. According to a research by Reichheld and Sasser in the Harvard Business Review, 5 per cent increase in customer retention can increase profitability by 35 per cent in hoteliering business, 50 per cent in insurance and brokerage, and 125 per cent in the consumer credit card market.

In the **"Timesaving services such as valet parking"** Chain hotels as well as standalone hotels have scored equally in this criterion and take initiatives in providing customers with good valet parking service. A good valet parking facility not only impress in house guest but also make an impression on people coming from outside like for banquet functions etc. the hotels have realized the importance of the same and so pay importance to it

When we see "**Floor concierge**", Standalone hotels have scored better by getting a score of 7.71 against 7.67 scored by Chain hotels. In hotels, a concierge assists guests with various tasks like making restaurant reservations, arranging for spa services, recommending night life hot spots, booking transportation (limousines, airplanes, boats, etc.), procurement of tickets to special events and assisting with various travel arrangements and tours of local attractions. In upscale establishments, a concierge is often expected to "achieve the impossible", dealing with any request a guest may have, no matter how strange, relying on an extensive list of contacts with local merchants and service providers. Concierge is a personalized service and the research show that Standalone hotels pay more attention on concierge service

In "**Provision of gym and other recreational facilities**" Chain hotels have scored better by getting a score of 8.03 against 7.90 scored by Standalone hotels. Chain hotels generally sign up with fitness companies to man their gym so the facility and quality of their gym is very high as compared to standalone properties who are not able to do the same

In the criteria "**Shops within the hotel**" Chain hotels have scored better by getting a score of 7.48 against 5.88 scored by Standalone hotels. We can see a remarkable difference in the score of hotels this may be because generally Chain hotels sign up with big retail brands to open shops on their premises in all their Chain properties where as the Standalone properties find it difficult to do so as they have only one property and the retailers don't find it profitable. Thus the number of shops in a standalone property is very less as compared to Chain hotels.

In **"High level of security"** Standalone hotels have scored better by getting a score of 7.92 against 7.81 scored by Chain hotels. Security has become a major concern of the hotels especially after the terrorist attack on Mumbai hotels. The research shows that the security levels in standalone properties are better. The reason is that being individual property it is easier to keep a track on guest and employees than Chain hotels as the numbers are limited and also the procedures and policies of the hotels can be molded to the need of the property

In the **"Overall Facilities of the Hotel"** Chain hotels have scored better by getting a score of 9.25 against 9.02 scored by Standalone hotels. Overall Chain hotels give a better impression as far as facilities is concerned

1.4.5.3 Dimension – Hotel Front office

$H_{2.3}$: There is no significant difference between service quality perceptions related to Hotel front office of Standalone and Chain Hotels.

Hotel Front office

Group Statistics

	Hotel	N	Mean	Std. Deviation	Std. Error Mean
Hotel Front Office	Chain	200	39.9050	5.84244	.41312
	Standalone	300	40.0067	6.03834	.34862

Independent Samples Test

		Levene's Test for Equality of Variances		t-test for Equality of Means					95% Confiden Interval Differen
		F	Sig.	t	df	Sig. (2-tailed)	Mean Difference	Std. Error Difference	Lower
Hotel Front office	Equal variances assumed	.240	.624	-.187	498	.852	-.10167	.54415	-1.17077
	Equal variances not assumed			-.188	436.138	.851	-.10167	.54056	-1.16410

The Mean of Chain Hotels was 39.905 and the standard deviation 5.842. The Mean of Standalone Hotels was 40.006 and the Standard Deviation 6.038. An Independent samples t-test was conducted to examine whether there was a significant difference between service quality perceptions of Hotel Front office between Customers of Standalone and Chain Hotels. The p-value (sig.) for the Levene's test . .624), is above .05, hence equal variances are assumed. The test revealed a statistically significant difference between Standalone and Chain Hotel Customers ($t = -.187$, $df = 498$ $p > .05$). Hence the hypothesis that that there is no significant difference in service quality perceptions of Hotel Front office between Standalone and Chain Hotel Customers is rejected. Hotel Front office of Standalone Hotels (mean = 40.006, sd = 6.038) is perceived to be of higher quality than Chain Hotels (mean = 39.905, sd = 5.842).

Mean of Individual Items under Hotel Front office

	Chain	Standalone
1. Check in & check out process	8.12	8.23
2. Bell desk service	8.18	8.18
3.Travel desk service	7.55	7.91
4. Billing accuracy	8.10	8.12
5. Airport service offered by the Hotel	7.97	7.57
Overall	7.98	8.00

If we compare the services provided by the front office of Chain hotels and Standalone Hotels, Standalone hotels have been perceived much better as compared to Chain Hotels like in the criteria "**Check in & check out process**" Standalone hotels have scored better by getting a score of 8.23 against 8.12 scored by Chain hotels. In the "**Travel desk service** "again the Standalone hotels have scored better by getting a score of 7.91 against 7.55   scored by Chain hotels. Also in "**Billing accuracy**" Standalone hotels have a better score of 8.12 as against 8.10 scored by Chain Hotels.

In the "**Bell desk service**" both the categories of hotels have scored equivalent of 8.18. The guest has perceived both equally well.

In the only criteria where Chain Hotels have done well is "**Airport service offered by the Hotel**" where Chain hotels have scored 7.97 as compared to 7.57 scored by

Standalone hotels. The guest have perceived the airport services of Chain Hotels to be better than Standalone.

If we see the **"Overall"** scoring of front office services of Chain Hotels and Standalone hotels, Chain hotels have performed poor or the guest have perceived Standalone hotels better by giving a score of 8.00 as compared to Chain hotels with a score of 7.98

1.4.5.4 Dimension - Room Product

$H_{2.4}$: There is no significant difference between service quality perceptions related to Room Product of Standalone and Chain Hotels.

Room Product

Group Statistics

	Hotel	N	Mean	Std. Deviation	Std. Error Mean
Room Product	Chain	200	53.6000	8.25230	.58353
	Standalone	300	55.1000	10.45695	.60373

Independent Samples Test

				t-test for Equality of Means						
Levene's Test for Equality of Variances									95% Confidence Interval of the Difference	
		F	Sig.	t	d f	Sig. (2-tailed)	Mean Differ ence	Std. Error Differenc e	Lower	Uppe r
Room Product	Equal variances assumed	.007	.933	-1.705	4 9 8	.089	- 1.5000 0	.87970	-3.22839	.2283 9
	Equal variances not assumed			-1.786	4 8 3. 9 7 3	.075	- 1.5000 0	.83964	-3.14979	.1497 9

The Mean of Chain Hotels was 53.600and the standard deviation 8.252. The Mean of Standalone Hotels was 55.10 and the Standard Deviation 10.456. An Independent samples t-test was conducted to examine whether there was a significant difference between service quality perceptions of Room Product between Customers of Standalone and Chain Hotels. The p-value (sig.) for the Levene's test . .933), is above .05, hence equal variances are assumed. The test revealed that there is a statistically significant difference between Standalone and Chain Hotel Customers (t = -1.705, df = 498 p >

.05). Hence the hypothesis that that there is no significant difference in service quality perceptions of Room Product between Standalone and Chain Hotel Customers is rejected. Room Product of Standalone Hotels (mean = 55.10, sd = 10.456) is perceived to be of higher quality than Chain Hotels (mean = 53.60, sd = 8.252).

Mean of Individual Items under Room Product

	Chain	Standalone
1. Large, comfortable beds	7.56	8.14
2. Luxurious branded toiletries	7.23	7.88
3. Linen quality	7.61	7.75
4. Range of toiletries available in the bathroom	7.54	7.60
5. Provision of stationery in the room	7.99	7.86
6. Spacious room and bathrooms	7.67	7.96
7. Deluxe appliances	8.03	7.92
Total	7.66	7.87

In providing "**Large, comfortable beds**" Standalone hotels have scored better by getting a score of 7.56 against 8.14 scored by Chain hotels. Their quality of bed have been perceived better by the guest as the quality of both mattress and bed is extremely good

In the criteria "**Luxurious branded toiletries**" Standalone hotels have scored better by getting a score of 7.88 against 7.23 scored by Chain hotels. The quality of branded toiletries provided by the Standalone hotels is much better than the Chain hotels. Chain hotels generally concentrate more on quantity and miss out on quality.

In providing **"Linen quality"** Standalone hotels have scored better by getting a score of 7.75 against 7.61 scored by Chain hotels. The number of towels as well as the quality of linen as compared to the Chain hotels, the Standalone hotels have been perceived better

In the criteria **"Range of toiletries available in the bathroom"** Standalone hotels have scored better by getting a score of 7.60 against 7.54 scored by Chain hotels.

When we see **"Provision of stationery in the room"** Chain hotels have scored better by getting a score of 7.99 against 7.86 scored by Standalone hotels. The reason being the personalized stationeries being used by Chain hotels which includes letter head with the guest name written etc. which is highly appreciated by the guest.

In keeping **"Deluxe appliances"** Chain hotels have scored extremely high a score of 8.03 against 7.92 scored by Standalone hotels   . The reason here is that the Chain hotels generally sign up with good brand to supply appliances for all their hotels at a cheap rate which the Standalone properties are unable to do, so they are not able to afford the appliances to be put in the rooms

In providing **"Spacious room and bathrooms"** Standalone hotels have scored better by getting a score of 7.96 against 7.67 scored by Chain hotels.

In providing **"Spacious room and bathrooms"** Standalone hotels have scored better by getting a score of 7.96 against 7.67 scored by Chain hotels.

If we see the "**Total**" score Standalone hotels have scored better by getting a score of 7.87 against 7.66 scored by Chain hotels.   The   reason   being   that   Standalone properties are able to concentrate more on individual need of the clientele and also most of their suppliers are local so they do not run short on supplies. They have pillow menus to provide variety of pillows and also for toiletries they are able to easily change them according to the season or need of the customer

1.4.5.5 Dimension - Food & Beverage Service

$H_{2.5}$: There is no significant difference between service quality perceptions related to Food & Beverage Service of Standalone and Chain Hotels.

Food & Beverage Service

Group Statistics

	Hotel	N	Mean	Std. Deviation	Std. Error Mean
FBP Servic e	Chain	200	56.5750	7.44726	.52660
	Standalon e	300	56.2900	10.30533	.59498

Independent Samples Test

				t-test for Equality of Means						
Levene's Test for Equality of Variances									**95% Confidence Interval of the Difference**	
		F	Sig.	t	df	Sig. (2-tailed)	Mean Differen ce	Std. Error Differenc e	Lower	Upper
FBP Service	Equal variance s assumed	.23 5	.62 8	.33 7	498	.736	.28500	.84619	- 1.3775 5	1.94755
	Equal variance s not assumed			.35 9	494 .75 6	.720	.28500	.79455	- 1.2761 1	1.84611

The Mean of Chain Hotels was 56.575 and the standard deviation 7.447. The Mean of Standalone Hotels was 56.290 and the Standard Deviation 10.305. An Independent samples t-test was conducted to examine whether there was a significant difference between service quality perceptions of Food & Beverage Service of Standalone and Chain Hotels. The p-value (sig.) for the Levene's test(.628) , is more than .05, hence equal variances are assumed. The test revealed that statistically there is a significant difference between Standalone and Chain Hotel Customers ($t = .337$, $df = 498$, $p > .05$).

Hence the hypothesis that that there is no significant difference in service quality perceptions of Food and beverage service between Standalone and Chain Hotel Customers is rejected. . Food & Beverage Service of the Hotel of Chain Hotels (mean = 56.575, sd = 7.447) is perceived to be of higher quality than Standalone Hotels (mean = 56.290, sd = 10.305).

Mean of Individual Items under Food and Beverage Service

	Chain	Standalo
1. Provision of a sumptuous buffet	8.40	8.05
2. Good range of bars to buy a drink	8.10	8.06
3. Staff knowledge of menu	7.77	7.87
4. Quality of service	8.01	8.05
5. Fairly priced food and beverage	8.13	8.02
6. Economical items available for room service	7.96	8.13
7. Affordability of items in the mini bar	8.23	8.12
Overall	8.08	8.04

In providing "**Provision of a sumptuous buffet** " Chain hotels have scored better by getting a score of 8.40 against 8.05 scored by Standalone hotels. They have also scored well in providing "**Good range of bars to buy a drink**" with scoring of 8.10 against 8.06 scored by Standalone hotels. Chain hotels have even scored high in providing "**Fairly priced food and beverage**", they have scored better by getting a score of 8.13 against 8.02 scored by Standalone hotels. And also in providing "**Affordability of items in the mini bar**" Chain hotels have scored better by getting a score of 8.23 against 8.12 scored by Standalone hotels.   In "**Overall food and beverage service**" Chain hotels have scored better by getting a score of 8.08 against 8.04 scored by Standalone hotels. This shows that in Chain Hotels provide bigger range of food and beverage products in restaurants, bars and minibar, and with better pricing whereas if we see the providing "**Staff knowledge of menu**" Standalone hotels have scored better by getting a score of 7.87 against 7.77 scored by Chain hotels. And also they have done well in providing "**Quality of service**" where Standalone hotels have scored better by getting a score of 8.05 against 8.01 scored by Chain hotels. "**Economical items available for room service**" Standalone hotels have scored better by getting a score of 8.13 against 7.96 scored by Chain hotels.

The scores show that where the Chain hotels have scored well in proving better variety of Food and Beverage Service, in the same place Standalone hotels have done extremely well in giving good food quality and staff knowledge of food. Both categories of hotels have showed their strong sides where the Chain hotels are concentrating more in variety and Standalone concentrate more on quality of food and beverage.

1.4.5.6 Dimension - Food & Beverage product

$H_{2.6}$: There is no significant difference between service quality perceptions related to Food & Beverage Product of Standalone and Chain Hotels.

Food & Beverage product

Group Statistics

Group Statistics						
	Hotel	N	Mean	Std. Deviation	Std. Error Mean	
FBP Product	Chain	200	39.9950	7.01362	.49594	
	Standalone	300	41.2833	5.99356	.34604	

Independent Samples Test

Levene's Test for Equality of Variances		F	Si g.	t	df	Sig. (2-tailed)	Mean Diffe rence	Std. Error Differe nce	95% Confiden Interval of Difference Lower	Upper
				t-test for Equality of Means						
FBP Product	Equal variances assumed	6.7 61	.0 1 0	- 2.1 98	498	.028	- 1.288 33	.58612	-2.43991	-.1367
	Equal variances not assumed			- 2.1 30	379.9 90	.034	- 1.288 33	.60473	-2.47737	-.0993

The Mean of Chain Hotels was 39.995 and the standard deviation 7.013. The Mean of Standalone Hotels was 41.283and the Standard Deviation 5.993. An Independent samples t-test was conducted to examine whether there was a significant difference between service quality perceptions of Food & Beverage Product of Standalone and Chain Hotels. The p-value (sig.) for the Levene's test(.010) , is less than .05, hence equal variances are not assumed. The test revealed that statistically there is no significant difference between Standalone and Chain Hotel Customers ($t = 2.130$, df = 379, $p < .05$). Hence the hypothesis that that there is no significant difference in service quality perceptions of Food & Beverage Product between Standalone and Chain Hotel Customers is accepted.

1.4.5.7 Dimension - Personalised Service

$H_{2.7}$: There is no significant difference between service quality perceptions related to Personalised Service of Standalone and Chain Hotels.

Personalised Service

Group Statistics

	Hotel	N	Mean	Std. Deviation	Std. Error Mean
Personalised service	Chain	200	40.6650	7.68427	.54336
	Stand alone	300	41.5567	9.38084	.54160

Independent Samples Test

				t-test for Equality of Means						
Levene's Test for Equality of Variances									95% Confidence Interval of the Difference	
		F	Sig.	t	df	Sig. (2-tailed)	Mean Difference	Std. Error Difference	Lower	Upper
Personalise d service	Equal variances assumed	.928	.336	- 1.1 17	498	.264	-.89167	.79808	-2.45968	.67634

			- 1.1 62	477. 294	.246	-.89167	.76719	-2.39915	.6
Equal variances not assumed									

The Mean of Chain Hotels was 40.665 and the standard deviation 41.556. The Mean of Standalone Hotels was 41.556 and the Standard Deviation 9.3808. An Independent samples t-test was conducted to examine whether there was a significant difference between service quality perceptions of Personalised Service of Standalone and Chain Hotels. The p-value (sig.) for the Levene's test (.336) is more than .05, hence equal variances are assumed. The test revealed that statistically there is a significant difference between Standalone and Chain Hotel Customers (t = -1.117 df = 498, p > .05). Hence the hypothesis that that there is no significant difference in service quality perceptions of Personalised Service between Standalone and Chain Hotel Customers is rejected. . Personalised Service of the Hotel of Standalone Hotels (mean =41.556, sd = 7.68427) is perceived to be of higher quality than Chain Hotels (mean = 40.665, sd = 9.38084).

Mean of Individual Items under Personalised Service

	Chain	Standa
1. Guest relation service	8.09	8.31
2. To be acknowledged rather than to be treated as just another customer	7.88	8.29
3. To be made to feel special	7.91	8.23
4. Staff remembering your requirements	8.28	8.24

5. The staff remember your name	8.51	8.48
Overall	8.13	8.31

In providing "**Guest relation service**" Standalone hotels have scored better by getting a score of 8.31against 8.09 scored by Chain hotels. Also in providing "**To be acknowledged rather than to be treated as just another customer**" Standalone hotels have scored better by a scoring 8.29 against 7.88 scored by Chain hotels. And in providing "**To be made to feel special**" also Standalone hotels have scored better by getting a score of 8.23 against 7.91 scored by Chain hotels. "**Overall**" Standalone hotels have scored better by getting a score of 8.31 against 8.13 scored by Chain hotels in the above mentioned criteria. Whereas in providing "**Staff remembering your requirements**" Chain hotels have scored better by getting a score of 8.28 against 8.24 scored by Standalone hotels.

And providing "**The staff remembers your name**" also Chain hotels have scored better by getting a score of 8.51 against 8.48 scored by Standalone hotels. This gives a clear picture that in providing personalized service guest perceives that Standalone hotels do a better job. A reason for this might be that the staff are well trained in performing their job. But when we see other criteria like "**Staff remembering your requirements**" and "**The staff remember your name**" Chain hotels have taken the lead. The reason for this might be that Chain hotels generally have a very good software which has a function called "guest history", where the staff fills in the details of guest likes and dislikes so that it can be remembered on his next visit. The same way the telephones also reflect the guest name when the guest call from rooms, so whoever picks up the calls can address guest by name.

1.4.5.8 Dimension – Service In General

$H_{2.8}$: There is no significant difference between service quality perceptions related to Service In General of Standalone and Chain Hotels.

Service In General

Group Statistics

	Hotel	N	Mean	Std. Deviation	Std. Mean
Service In General	Chain	200	40.4400	6.39617	.45228
	Standalone	300	39.9233	5.25447	.30337

Independent Samples Test

					t-test for Equality of Means				
Levene's Test for Equality of Variances									95% Confidence Interval of the Difference
		F	Sig.	t	df	Sig. (2-tailed)	Mean Differen ce	Std. Error Differenc e	Lower
Service In General	Equal variance s	4.631	.03 2	.986	49 8	.324	.51667	.52381	-.51248

	assumed									
	Equal variance s not assumed			.949	36 8.6 78	.343	.51667	.54460	-.55424	1.5875 7

The Mean of Chain Hotels was 40.440 and the standard deviation 6.396. The Mean of Standalone Hotels was 39.923 and the Standard Deviation 5.254. An Independent samples t-test was conducted to examine whether there was a significant difference between service quality perceptions of Service In General of Standalone and Chain Hotels. The p-value (sig.) for the Levene's test (.332) is more than .05, hence equal variances are assumed. The test revealed that statistically there is significant difference between Standalone and Chain Hotel Customers (t = .986 df = 498, p > .05). Hence the hypothesis that that there is no significant difference in service quality perceptions of Service In General between Standalone and Chain Hotel Customers is rejected. . Service In General of the Hotel of Chain Hotels (mean =40.440, sd = 6.396) is perceived to be of higher quality than Standalone Hotels (mean = 39.923, sd = 5.254).

Mean of Individual Items under Service in general

	Chain	Standalone
1. Not being kept waiting for more than a minute	8.13	8.14
2. Immediate service	8.03	7.95
3. Every need is anticipated	7.76	8.05
4. Precise attention to detail	8.07	8.14
5. Professional service	8.46	8.04
Overall	8.09	7.98

In providing "**Not being kept waiting for more than a minute**" Standalone hotels have scored better by getting a score 8.14 of against 8.13 scored by Chain hotels. Also in providing "**Every need is anticipated**" Standalone hotels have scored better by getting a score 8.05 of against 7.76 scored by Chain hotels. And in providing "**Precise attention to detail**" Standalone hotels have scored better by getting a score 8.14 of against 8.07scored by Chain hotels.

In providing "**Immediate service**" Chain hotels have scored better by getting a score of 8.03 against 7.95 scored by Standalone hotels. Also in providing "**Professional service**" Chain hotels have scored better by getting a score of 8.46 against 8.04 scored by Standalone hotels. But if we see "**Overall**" Chain hotels have scored better by getting a score of 8.09 against 7.98 scored by Standalone hotels.

Here we can see a big difference in the guest perception of service in general between Chain hotels and Standalone hotels. The guest perceives that the Chain hotels give immediate and professional service as compared to Standalone hotels. The reason for the same can be better training of staff and better use of technology

1.4.5.9 Dimension – Hotel staff

$H_{2.9}$: There is no significant difference between service quality perceptions related to Hotel staff of Standalone and Chain Hotels.

Hotel staff

Group Statistics

	Hotel	N	Mean	Std. Deviation	Std. Error Mea
Hotel staff	**Chain**	200	40.4050	6.61797	.467
	Standalone	300	40.2900	5.81595	.335

Independent Samples Test

Levene's Test for Equality of Variances				t-test for Equality of Means					95% Confidence Interval of the Difference	
		F	Sig.	T	df	Sig. (2-tailed)	Mean Difference	Std. Error Difference	Lower	Upper
Hotel Staff	Equal variances assumed	2.787	.096	.205	498	.838	.11500	.56132	-.98786	1.21786
	Equal variances not assumed			.200	388.185	.842	.11500	.57597	-1.01741	1.24741

The Mean of Chain Hotels was 40.405 and the standard deviation 6.617. The Mean of Standalone Hotels was 40.290 and the Standard Deviation 5.815. An Independent samples t-test was conducted to examine whether there was a significant difference between service quality perceptions of Hotel Staff of Standalone and Chain Hotels. The p-value (sig.) for the Levene's test (.096) is more than .05, hence equal variances are assumed. The test revealed that statistically there is significant difference between Standalone and Chain Hotel Customers (t = .205 df = 498, p > .05). Hence the hypothesis that that there is no significant difference in service quality perceptions of Hotel staff between Standalone and Chain Hotel Customers is rejected. . Hotel staff of Chain Hotels (mean =40.405, sd = 6.617) is perceived to be of higher quality than Standalone Hotels (mean = 40.290, sd = 5.815).

Mean of Individual Items under Hotel Staff

	Chain	Standalone
1. Staff who understand and meet unusual requests	8.10	8.07
2. High quality staff who are well trained	8.24	8.28
3. Smiling and friendly staff	8.31	8.16
4. Staff who anticipate your needs	7.96	7.84
5. Staff who understand classy patrons	7.81	7.93
Overall	8.08	8.06

In providing "**Staff who understand and meet unusual requests**" Chain hotels have scored better by getting a score of 8.10 against 8.07 scored by Standalone hotels. Also in providing "**Smiling and friendly staff**" Chain hotels have scored better by getting a score of 8.31 against 8.16 scored by Standalone hotels. And in providing "**Staff who anticipate your needs**" Chain hotels have scored better by getting a score of 7.96 against 7.84 scored by Standalone hotels. Whereas in providing "**High quality staff who are well trained**" Standalone hotels have scored better by getting a score of 8.28 against 8.24 scored by Chain hotels. And in providing "**Staff who understand classy patrons**" Standalone hotels have scored better by getting a score of 7.93 against 7.81

scored by Chain hotels. "**Overall**" Chain hotels have scored better by getting a score of 8.08 against 8.06 scored by Standalone hotels. It clearly indicates that as far as Hotel staff is concerned Chain hotels have been perceived better by guests. This criteria highlights the training capabilities of a hotel where the Chain hotels have surpassed the Standalone hotels.

1.4.5.10 Dimension – Overall service quality

$H_{2.10}$: There is no significant difference between service quality perceptions related to Overall service quality of Standalone and Chain Hotels.

Overall service quality

Group Statistics

	Hotel	N	Mean	Std. Deviation	Std. Error Mean
Overall service quality	Chain	200	316.5500	34.22146	2.41982
	Standalone	300	318.2667	45.96249	2.65365

Independent Samples Test

				t-test for Equality of Means						
Levene's Test for Equality of Variances									95% Confidence Interval of the Difference	
		F	Sig.	t	df	Sig. (2-tailed)	Mean Difference	Std. Error Difference	Lower	Uppr
Overall service quality	Equal variances assumed	.207	.649	-.451	498	.652	-1.71667	3.80389	-9.19032	5.74 99
	Equal variances not assumed			-.478	491.930	.633	-1.71667	3.59129	-8.77283	5.33 50

The Mean of Chain Hotels was 316.550 and the standard deviation 34.221. The Mean of Standalone Hotels was 318.266 and the Standard Deviation 45.962. An Independent samples t-test was conducted to examine whether there was a significant difference between overall service quality of Standalone and Chain Hotels. The p-value (sig.) for the Levene's test (.649) is more than .05, hence equal variances are assumed. The test revealed that statistically there is significant difference between Standalone and Chain Hotel Customers (t = -.451 df = 498, p > .05). Hence the hypothesis that that there is no significant difference in overall service quality between Standalone and Chain Hotel Customers is rejected. . Overall service quality of Standalone Hotels (mean =318.266, sd = 45.962) is perceived to be of higher quality than Chain Hotels (mean = 316.550, sd = 34.221).

Mean of Individual Items under Overall service quality

	Chain	Standalone
Presentation	7.73	8.00
Facilities of the Hotel	7.71	7.52
Hotel Front Office	7.98	8.00
Room Product	7.66	7.87
Food & Beverage Service	8.08	8.04
Food and Beverage production	8.00	8.26
Personalised Service	8.13	8.31
Service In General	8.09	7.98
Hotel Staff	8.08	8.06
Overall	7.93	7.99

In providing "**Facilities of the Hotel**" Chain hotels have scored better by getting a score of 7.71 against 7.52 scored by Standalone hotels. And in providing "**Food & Beverage service**" Chain hotels have scored better by getting a score of 8.08 against 8.04 scored by Standalone hotels. Also in providing "**Service In General**" Chain hotels have scored better by getting a score of 8.09 against 7.98 scored by Standalone hotels. And in providing **"Hotel Staff"** Chain hotels have scored better by getting a score of 8.08 against 8.06 scored by Standalone hotels.

Whereas in providing **"Presentation"** Standalone hotels have scored better by getting a score of 8.00 against 7.73 scored by Chain hotels. And in providing **"Room Product"** Standalone hotels have scored better by getting a score of 7.87against 7.66 scored by Chain hotels. Also in providing **"Personalised Service"** Standalone hotels have scored better by getting a score of 8.31 against 8.13 scored by Chain hotels. In the criteria **"Food & Beverage Product"** Standalone hotels have scored better by getting a score of 8.26 against 8.00 scored by Chain hotels. In the quality of **"Hotel Front office"** Standalone hotels have scored better by getting a score of 8.00 against 7.98 scored by Chain hotels.

When we see **"Overall Hotel"** Standalone hotels have scored better by getting a score of 7.99 against 7.93 scored by Chain hotels. Overall the guests have perceived Standalone hotels better than Chain hotels. Standalone hotels pay more attention to location of the hotel also their presentation is better perceived than Chain hotel. Their rooms and amenities are much better and also they are able to give much personalized service. The front office facilities and the food product are perceived much better by guest than as compared to Chain Hotels.

1.4.6 To Compare Service Quality Gaps (Gap-5): (Customer Expected – Customer Perceived) of Chain Hotels and Standalone Hotels.

The difference between what customers expect of a service and what they actually receive is Gap 5 of the Servqual Model. Customer expectations are shaped from word of mouth, their personal needs and their own past experiences. The perception is the result of the actual service delivery encounter experience.

1.4.6.1 Gap 5 in Dimension – Presentation of the Hotel

$H_{3.1}$: There is no significant difference in service quality gaps (Customer Expected - Customer Perceived) relating to Presentation of Chain Hotels and Standalone Hotels.

Presentation of the Hotel

Group Statistics

	Hotel	N	Mean	Std. Deviation	Std. Error Mean
Presentation	Chain	200	6.0200	7.02183	.49652
	Standalone	300	2.8267	6.41564	.37041

Independent Samples Test

		Levene's Test for Equality of Variances		t-test for Equality of Means					95% Confidence Interval of the Difference	
		F	Sig.	t	df	Sig. (2-tailed)	Mean Difference	Std. Error Difference	Lower	Upper
Presentation	Equal variances assumed	3.627	.057	5.249	498	.000	3.19333	.60838	1.998 02	4.3886 5
	Equal variances not assumed			5.155	399.734	.000	3.19333	.61946	1.975 52	4.4111 4

The Mean of Chain Hotels was 6.020 and the standard deviation 7.021. The Mean of Standalone Hotels was 2.826 and the Standard Deviation 6.415. An Independent samples t-test was conducted to examine whether there was a significant difference in Service Quality Gaps (expected and perceived by Customers) with regard to presentation of Standalone and Chain Hotels. The p-value (sig.) for the Levene's test .057), is above .05, hence equal variances are assumed. The test revealed that statistically there is no significant difference in Service Quality Gaps (expected and perceived by Customers) with regard to presentation of Standalone and Chain Hotel Customers (t = 5.249, df = 498 p <.05). Hence the hypothesis that that there is no significant difference in Service Quality Gaps (expected and perceived by Customers) with regard to Presentation of the Hotel between Standalone and Chain Hotel Customers is accepted

1.4.6.2 Gap 5 in Dimension – Facilities of the Hotel

$H_{3.2}$: There is no significant difference in service quality gaps (Customer Expected - Customer Perceived) relating to Facilities of the Hotel of Chain Hotels and Standalone Hotels.

Presentation of the Hotel

Group Statistics

	Hotel	N	Mean	Std. Deviation	Std. Error Mean
Facilities of the Hotel	Chain	200	6.1250	10.02268	.70871
	Standalone	300	4.7467	7.72364	.44592

Independent Samples Test

		Levene's Test for Equality of Variances		t-test for Equality of Means					95% Confidence Interval of the Difference	
		F	Sig.	t	df	Sig. (2-tailed)	Mean Difference	Std. Error Difference	Lower	Upper
Facilities of the Hotel	Equal variances assumed	19.520	.000	1.732	498	.084	1.37833	.79560	-.18482	2.94149
	Equal variances not assumed			1.646	351.130	.101	1.37833	.83733	-.26848	3.02514

The Mean of Chain Hotels was 6.125 and the standard deviation 10.022. The Mean of Standalone Hotels was 4.746 and the Standard Deviation 7.723. An Independent samples t-test was conducted to examine whether there was a significant difference in Service Quality Gaps (expected and perceived by Customers) with regard to presentation of Standalone and Chain Hotels. The p-value (sig.) for the Levene's test .000), is below .05, hence equal variances are not assumed. The test revealed that statistically there is a significant difference in Service Quality Gaps (expected and perceived by Customers) with regard to presentation of Standalone and Chain Hotel Customers (t = 1.646, df = 351.13 p >.05). Hence the hypothesis that that there is no significant difference in Service Quality Gaps (expected and perceived by Customers) with regard to Presentation of the Hotel between Standalone and Chain Hotel

Customers is rejected. Service Quality Gap with regard to Facilities of Chain Hotels (mean =6.125, sd = 10.022) is more than Standalone Hotels (mean = 4.746, sd = 7.723).

Gap scores of Individual items under

Facilities of the Hotel

	Chain	Standalone
1. Fabulous views from the hotel room	-0.91	-0.68
2. Timesaving services such as valet parking	-1.24	-0.41
3. Floor concierge	-1.60	-0.77
4. Provision of gym and other recreational facilities	-1.28	-0.93
5. Shops within the hotel	-0.71	0.80
6. High level of security	-0.90	-0.72
Overall	-1.11	-0.45

Both Chain Hotels and Standalone Hotels have failed to meet the customer's expectation in most of the sub-elements of Facilities in the Hotel. The modern guest expects a lot as far as facilities of the hotels is concerned. The customer expects an overall package from the hotel wherein the hotel should have a good view, a good valet parking, and recreational facility and with all this a high level of security. The above gap reflects that both Chain Hotels and Standalone hotels do not provide apt facilities expected by the guest. Only in providing shops within the Hotel standalone hotels have exceeded the expectation of the guest by providing shops on premises for guest use. The Hotels need to work a lot as far as facilities are concerned as the gap between expectation of the guest and perception of the guest is very high.

1.4.6.3 Gap 5 in Dimension – Hotel Front Office

$H_{3.3}$: There is no significant difference in service quality gaps (Customer Expected - Customer Perceived) relating to Hotel Front Office of Chain Hotels and Standalone Hotels.

Hotel Front Office

Group Statistics

	Hotel	N	Mean	Std. Deviation	Std. Error Mean
Hotel Front Office	Chain	200	4.9950	7.52066	.53179
	Standalone	300	3.9167	5.45671	.31504

Independent Samples Test

		Levene's Test for Equality of Variances		t-test for Equality of Means					95% Confidence Interval of the Difference	
		F	Sig.	t	df	Sig. (2-tailed)	Mean Differ-ence	Std. Error Differ-ence	Lower	Upper
Hotel Front Office	Equal variances assumed	3.847	.051	1.857	498	.064	1.07833	.58079	-.06278	2.21944
	Equal variances not assumed			1.745	335.676	.082	1.07833	.61810	-.13751	2.29418

The Mean of Chain Hotels was 4.995 and the standard deviation is 7.520. The Mean of Standalone Hotels was 3.916 and the Standard Deviation 5.456. An Independent samples t-test was conducted to examine whether there was a significant difference in Service Quality Gaps (expected and perceived by Customers) with regard to Hotel Front office of Standalone and Chain Hotels. The p-value (sig.) for the Levene's test .051), is greater than .05, hence equal variances are assumed. The test revealed that statistically there is a significant difference in Service Quality Gaps (expected and perceived by Customers) with regard to presentation of Standalone and Chain Hotel Customers (t = 1.857, df = 498 p >.05). Hence the hypothesis that that there is no significant difference in Service Quality Gaps (expected and perceived by Customers) with regard to Hotel Front office between Standalone and Chain Hotel Customers is rejected. Service Quality Gap with regard to Front office of Chain Hotels (mean =4.995, sd = 7.520) is more than Standalone Hotels (mean = 3.916, sd = 5.456).

Gap scores of Individual items under

Hotel Front office

	Chain	Standalone
1. Check in & check out process	0.96	0.72
2. Bell desk service	0.95	0.76
3. Travel desk service	1.52	0.82
4. Billing accuracy	0.81	0.68
5. Airport service offered by the Hotel	0.77	0.93
Overall	1.00	0.78

Front office is the face of the hotel and it is very important that the Hotel front office is good as it creates the first impression of the hotel on the guests. Both Chain Hotels and Standalone Hotels have exceeded to meet the guest's expectation in all the sub-elements of Hotel Front Office. It is relevant from the table that both the Chain Hotels as well as Standalone Hotels give equal importance to the front office and so have exceeded guest expectations

1.4.6.4 Gap 5 in Dimension – Room Product

$H_{3.4}$: There is no significant difference in service quality gaps (Customer Expected - Customer Perceived) relating to Room Product of Chain Hotels and Standalone Hotels.

Room Product

Group Statistics

	Hotel	N	Mean	Std. Deviation	Std. Error Mean
Room Product	**Chain**	200	7.8800	11.12720	.78681
	Standalone	300	5.3000	9.85123	.56876

Independent Samples Test										
				t-test for Equality of Means						
Levene's Test for Equality of Variances									95% Confidenc Interval the Difference	
		F	Sig.	t	df	Sig. (2-taile d)	Mean Differe nce	Std. Error Differen ce	Lowe r	U pe
Room Product	Equal variance s assumed	5.8 01	.01 6	2.72 3	498	.007	2.5800 0	.94755	.7183 0	4. 4 0
	Equal variance s not assumed			2.65 7	390. 366	.008	2.5800 0	.97086	.6712 4	4. 88 6

The Mean of Chain Hotels was 7.880 and the standard deviation 11.127. The Mean of Standalone Hotels was 5.300 and the Standard Deviation 9.851. An Independent samples t-test was conducted to examine whether there was a significant difference in Service Quality Gaps (expected and perceived by Customers) with regard to Room Product of Standalone and Chain Hotels. The p-value (sig.) for the Levene's test .016), is below .05, hence equal variances are not assumed. The test revealed that statistically there is a no significant difference in Service Quality Gaps (expected and perceived by Customers) with regard to presentation of Standalone and Chain Hotel Customers (t = 2.657, df = 390.36 p <.05). Hence the hypothesis that that there is no significant difference in Service Quality Gaps (expected and perceived by Customers) with regard to Room Product of the Hotel between Standalone and Chain Hotel Customers is accepted.

1.4.6.5 Gap 5 in Dimension – Food and Beverage Service

$H_{3.5}$: There is no significant difference in service quality gaps (Customer Expected - Customer Perceived) relating to Food and Beverage Service of Chain Hotels and Standalone Hotels.

Food and Beverage Service

Group Statistics

	Hotel	N	Mean	Std. Deviation	Std. Error Mean
Food and Beverage Service	Chain	200	8.3100	9.69245	.68536
	Standalone	300	4.2567	9.65201	.55726

Independent Samples Test

		Levene's Test for Equality of Variances		t-test for Equality of Means					95% Confidence Interval of the Difference	
		F	Sig.	t	df	Sig. (2-tailed)	Mean Difference	Std. Error Difference	Lower	Upper
Food and Beverage Service	Equal variances assumed	1.737	.188	4.593	498	.000	4.05333	.88258	2.319 29	5.7873 7

	Equal variances not assumed			4.58 9	425.36 5	.000	4.05333	.88332	2.317 12	5 5

The Mean of Chain Hotels was 8.310 and the standard deviation 9.692. The Mean of Standalone Hotels was 4.256 and the Standard Deviation 9.652. An Independent samples t-test was conducted to examine whether there was a significant difference in Service Quality Gaps (expected and perceived by Customers) with regard to Food and Beverage Service of Standalone and Chain Hotels. The p-value (sig.) for the Levene's test .188), is above .05, hence equal variances are assumed. The test revealed that statistically there is a no significant difference in Service Quality Gaps (expected and perceived by Customers) with regard to Food and Beverage Service of Standalone and Chain Hotel Customers (t = 4.593, df = 498 p <.05). Hence the hypothesis that that there is no significant difference in Service Quality Gaps (expected and perceived by Customers) with regard to Food and Beverage Service of the Hotel between Standalone and Chain Hotel Customers is accepted.

1.4.6.6 Gap 5 in Dimension – Food and Beverage Product

H[3.6]: There is no significant difference in service quality gaps (Customer Expected - Customer Perceived) relating to Food and Beverage Product of Chain Hotels and Standalone Hotels.

Food and Beverage Product

Group Statistics

	Hotel	N	Mean	Std. Deviation	Std. Error Mean
Food and Beverage Product	Chain	200	5.0650	8.42784	.59594
	Standalone	300	4.0233	6.25886	.36136

Independent Samples Test

		Levene's Test for Equality of Variances			t-test for Equality of Means					95% Confidence Interval of the Difference	
		F	Sig.	t	df	Sig. (2-tailed)	Mean Differenc e	Std. Error Differenc e	Lowe r	Upper
Food and Beverage Product	Equal variances assumed	19.0 55	.00 0	1.58 4	498	.114	1.04167	.65766	-.2504 7	2.3338 0
	Equal variances not assumed			1.49 5	341.51 1	.136	1.04167	.69694	-.3291 6	2.4124 9

The Mean of Chain Hotels was 5.065 and the standard deviation 8.427. The Mean of Standalone Hotels was 4.023 and the Standard Deviation 6.258. An Independent samples t-test was conducted to examine whether there was a significant difference in Service Quality Gaps (expected and perceived by Customers) with regard to Food and Beverage Product of Standalone and Chain Hotels. The p-value (sig.) for the Levene's test .000), is below .05, hence equal variances are not assumed. The test revealed that statistically there is a significant difference in Service Quality Gaps (expected and perceived by Customers) with regard to Food and Beverage Product of Standalone and Chain Hotel Customers (t = 1.495, df = 451.51 p >.05). Hence the hypothesis that that there is no significant difference in Service Quality Gaps (expected and perceived by Customers) with regard to Food and Beverage Product of the Hotel between Standalone and Chain Hotel Customers is rejected. Service Quality Gap with regard to Food and

Beverage Product of Chain Hotels (mean =5.065, sd = 8.427) is more than Standalone Hotels (mean = 4.023, sd = 6.258).

Gap scores of Individual items under

Food and Beverage Product

	Chain	Standalone
1. Quality of food	1.09	0.76
2. Exquisite food presentation	0.81	0.59
3. Taste of food	1.02	0.94
4. Portion size of dishes	1.15	1.01
5. Provision of live counters	1.02	0.72
Overall	1.01	0.80

Food and beverage product of any Hotel is the key to its success. As we can see from the table above, both the Chain Hotels as well as Standalone Hotels have exceeded guest expectation in giving good food. From providing good quality of food, giving exquisite food presentation, providing tasty food with good portion size of dishes to providing of live counters, hotels have exceeded the guest expectations and giving excellent service

1.4.6.7 Gap 5 in Dimension – Personalized Service

$H_{3.7}$: There is no significant difference in service quality gaps (Customer Expected - Customer Perceived) relating to Personalized Service of Chain Hotels and Standalone Hotels.

Personalized Service

Group Statistics

	Hotel	N	Mean	Std. Deviation	Std. Error Mean
Personalized Service	Chain	200	4.7050	9.15695	.64749
	Standalone	300	2.6033	5.93380	.34259

Independent Samples Test

				t-test for Equality of Means					
Levene's Test for Equality of Variances								95% Confidence Interval of the Difference	
		F	Sig.	t	df	Sig. (2-tailed)	Mean Difference	Std. Error Difference	Lower	Upper
Personalized Service	Equal variances assumed	18.601	.000	3.114	498	.002	2.10167	.67482	.77582	3.42752
	Equal variances not assumed			2.869	309.852	.004	2.10167	.73254	.66028	3.54305

The Mean of Chain Hotels was 4.705 and the standard deviation 9.156. The Mean of Standalone Hotels was 2.603 and the Standard Deviation 5.933. An Independent samples t-test was conducted to examine whether there was a significant difference in Service Quality Gaps (expected and perceived by Customers) with regard to Personalized Service of Standalone and Chain Hotels. The p-value (sig.) for the Levene's test .000), is below .05, hence equal variances are not assumed. The test revealed that statistically there is no significant difference in Service Quality Gaps (expected and perceived by Customers) with regard to Personalized Service of Standalone and Chain Hotel Customers (t = 2.869, df = 309.85 p <.05). Hence the hypothesis that that there is no significant difference in Service Quality Gaps (expected and perceived by Customers) with regard to Personalized Service of the Hotel between Standalone and Chain Hotel Customers is accepted.

1.4.6.8 Gap 5 in Dimensions – Service in General

$H_{3.8}$: There is no significant difference in service quality gaps (Customer Expected - Customer Perceived) relating to Service in General of Chain Hotels and Standalone Hotels.

Personalized Service

Group Statistics

	Hotel	N	Mean	Std. Deviation	Std. Error Mean
Service in General	Chain	200	4.5500	8.09228	.57221
	Standalone	300	5.0400	6.27239	.36214

Independent Samples Test

	t-test for Equality of Means	
		95%

Levene's Test for Equality of Variances		F	Sig.	t	df	Sig. (2-tailed)	Mean Difference	Std. Error Difference	Confidence Interval of the Difference	
									Lower	Upper
Service in General	Equal variances assumed	18.601	.000	3.114	498	.002	2.10167	.67482	.77582	3.42752
	Equal variances not assumed			2.869	309.852	.004	2.10167	.73254	.66028	3.54305

The Mean of Chain Hotels was 4.550 and the standard deviation 8.092. The Mean of Standalone Hotels was 5.040 and the Standard Deviation 6.272. An Independent samples t-test was conducted to examine whether there was a significant difference in Service Quality Gaps (expected and perceived by Customers) with regard to Service in General of Standalone and Chain Hotels. The p-value (sig.) for the Levene's test .000), is below .05, hence equal variances are not assumed. The test revealed that statistically there is a significant difference in Service Quality Gaps (expected and perceived by Customers) with regard to Service in General of Standalone and Chain Hotel Customers (t = 2.869, df = 309.85 p <.05). Hence the hypothesis that that there is no significant difference in Service Quality Gaps (expected and perceived by Customers) with regard to Service in General of the Hotel between Standalone and Chain Hotel Customers is rejected. Service Quality Gap with regard to Service in General of Standalone Hotels (mean = 5.0400, sd = 6.272) is more than Chain Hotels (mean = 4.550, sd = 8.092)

Gap scores of Individual items under

Service in General

	Chain	Standalone
1. Not being kept waiting for more than a minute	-0.88	-0.67
2. Immediate service	-1.17	-1.12
3. Every need is anticipated	-1.14	-1.02
4. Precise attention to detail	-0.71	-1.26
5. Professional service	-0.65	-0.96
Overall	-0.91	-1.26

It is relevant from the table that both Chain hotels and Standalone Hotels have failed in meeting guest expectations in providing service in general. The Gap between expected and perceived service quality is more in Standalone hotels as compared to Chain Hotels. This clearly indicates that as far as service in general is concerned the standalone Hotels need to pay more attention to details, give more professional and speedy service. As far as chain Hotels are concerned they need to pay more attention to anticipate guest need rather than the guest waiting for it. Today's guests are busy and have no time for waiting for any services and if the hotels want to excel themselves to other hotels they will have to focus more on speedy, accurate service with attention to detail.

1.4.6.9 Gap 5 in Dimension – Hotel Staff

$H_{3.9}$: There is no significant difference in service quality gaps (Customer Expected - Customer Perceived) relating to Hotel Staff of Chain Hotels and Standalone Hotels.

Hotel Staff

Group Statistics

	Hotel	N	Mean	Std. Deviation	Std. Error Mean
Hotel Staff	Chain	200	4.9550	7.40335	.52350
	Standalone	300	4.1967	6.47077	.37359

Independent Samples Test

		Levene's Test for Equality of Variances		t-test for Equality of Means						95% Confidence Interval of the Difference	
		F	Sig.	t	df	Sig. (2-tailed)	Mean Difference	Std. Error Difference	Lower	Upper
Hotel Staff	Equal variances assumed	.259	.611	1.211	498	.226	.75833	.62611	-.47180	1.98847
	Equal variances not assumed			1.179	386.579	.239	.75833	.64313	-.50614	2.02281

The Mean of Chain Hotels was 4.955 and the standard deviation 7.403. The Mean of Standalone Hotels was 4.196 and the Standard Deviation 6.470. An Independent samples t-test was conducted to examine whether there was a significant difference in Service Quality Gaps (expected and perceived by Customers) with regard to Hotel Staff of Standalone and Chain Hotels. The p-value (sig.) for the Levene's test .611), is above .05, hence equal variances are assumed. The test revealed that statistically there is a significant difference in Service Quality Gaps (expected and perceived by Customers) with regard to Hotel Staff of Standalone and Chain Hotel Customers (t = 1.211, df = 498 p >.05). Hence the hypothesis that that there is no significant difference in Service Quality Gaps (expected and perceived by Customers) with regard to Hotel Staff between Standalone and Chain Hotel Customers is rejected. Service Quality Gap with regard to Hotel Staff of Chain Hotels (mean =4.955, sd =7.403) is more than Standalone Hotels (mean = 4.196, sd = 6.470).

Gap scores of Individual items under

Hotel Staff

	Chain	Standa
1. Staff who understand and meet unusual requests	-1.03	-0.73
2. High quality staff who are well trained	-0.97	-0.88
3. Smiling and friendly staff	-1.60	-0.89
4. Staff who anticipate your needs	-0.78	-0.67
5. Staff who understand classy patrons	-1.08	-1.32
Overall	-1.09	-0.90

The Gap between expected and perceived service quality is more in Chain Hotels than Standalone Hotels. Hotel industry is a service industry and the services are rendered by staff. Overall if we look at the figures it clearly indicates that the hotels have failed in meeting guest expectation as far as staff is concerned. One of the prime reasons of this can be the high turnover of staff in the Hotel industry and also lack of skilled labour. Training also plays a key role as far as staff performance is concerned. The hotel industry altogether is lagging in providing good, professional and trained staff to deliver better service.

1.4.6.10 Gap 5 in Dimension – Overall Service Quality

$H_{3.10}$: There is no significant difference in service quality gaps (Customer Expected - Customer Perceived) relating to Overall Service Quality of Chain Hotels and Standalone Hotels.

Overall Service Quality

Group Statistics

	Hotel	N	Mean	Std. Deviation	Std. Error Mean
Overall Service Quality	Chain	200	49.3600	59.09774	4.17884
	Standalone	300	36.6767	48.15192	2.78005

Independent Samples Test

		Levene's Test for Equality of Variances		t-test for Equality of Means					95% Confidence Interval of the Difference	
		F	Sig.	t	df	Sig. (2-tailed)	Mean Difference	Std. Error Difference	Lower	Upper
Overall Service	Equal variances	13.200	.000	2.631	498	.009	12.68333	4.81985	3.21359	22.15307

Quality	assumed								
	Equal variances not assumed			2.52 7	366. 366	.02	12.68333	5.01910	2.81346

The Mean of Chain Hotels was 49.360 and the standard deviation 59.097. The Mean of Standalone Hotels was 36.676 and the Standard Deviation 48.151. An Independent samples t-test was conducted to examine whether there was a significant difference in Service Quality Gaps (expected and perceived by Customers) with regard to Overall Service Quality of Standalone and Chain Hotels. The p-value (sig.) for the Levene's test .000), is below .05, hence equal variances are not assumed. The test revealed that statistically there is no significant difference in Service Quality Gaps (expected and perceived by Customers) with regard to Overall Service Quality of Standalone and Chain Hotel Customers (t = 2.527, df = 366.36 p <.05). Hence the hypothesis that that there is no significant difference in Service Quality Gaps (expected and perceived by Customers) with regard to **Overall Service Quality** of the Hotel between Standalone and Chain Hotel Customers is rejected.

Gap scores of Individual items under

Overall Service Quality

	Chain	Standalone
Presentation	-1.20	-0.57
Overall Hotel	-1.02	-0.79
Room Product	-1.13	-0.76
Food & Beverage Product	-1.19	-0.61
Personalised Service	-0.94	-0.52
Service In General	-0.91	-1.01
Hotel Staff	-0.99	-0.84

HFO	-1.00	-0.78
FBP	-1.01	-0.80
Overall	-1.05	-0.74

If we see the overall score the Gap between expected service and perceived service quality is more in Chain Hotels than Standalone Hotels.

Except for the criteria service in general, in all the other criteria standalone hotels have scored fairly well as compared to chain hotel. This gives a clear cut picture that the customer expectation from the chain hotel is not met. The expectation is very high and the service perceived is very low.

When we see standalone hotels, even here the hotels have been perceived poor in most of the criteria.

CHAPTER 1.5
SUMMARY AND CONCLUSIONS

This research provides a valuable contribution to understanding the relationships that exist between the dimensions evaluated. The hotel industry is becoming progressively more competitive as the context of travel becomes more global and the industry structure changes. The research has value, not only in an academic context, but also for hotel managers at the unit and group level. Whilst several elements of the overall research model have been evaluated previously the overall model has not been examined.

In this study, a scale for measuring the service quality of five star hotels was proposed through exploratory factor analyses. Having knowledge on these areas would definitely help managers meet the challenge of improving service quality in the hotel industry. The current paper contributes to the theoretical orientation of tourism service quality and tourists' satisfaction in hotel industry literature by determining some pivotal service quality levels.

The results support the idea that despite the usefulness of the SERVQUAL scale as a concept, it should be adapted for the service environment as well. Along with the important findings obtained in this study, the modified questionnaire itself is another important contribution. The questionnaire developed through this study is suitable for use for guests staying in star hotels in India, allowing them to confidently identify the service areas of services which require action. At the same time, the modified questionnaire could also provide indicators through which managers and planners can plan service policies that would result in satisfied customers. Finally, the results of this study may not have been representative of the whole population, due to the fact that a convenience sampling method was used to collect the data. This study was conducted for only star hotels. To be able to generalize the findings for this specific hotel segment, a study that would include more hotels in a variety of regional settings could be conducted. Monitoring customer loyalty has become an important focus for all managers in the hotel industry. Failure to recognize the power of customer satisfaction, especially their emotions, could destroy the power of customer retention and loyalty.

Therefore, the hotel management's greatest challenge lies not only on attracting customers but specifically on identifying customer satisfaction individually. Customers may agree that the hotel provides high levels of service quality but not necessarily agree that the hotel ensures high satisfaction. Higher levels of quality are only meaningful to the extent that customers believe that value is being enhanced. Therefore, managers must carefully execute competition and understand the value perceived by different market segments. For example customers may sometimes refrain from purchasing when price is perceived to be too high, while some became suspicious of quality when price is too low. In summary, understanding the relationship among service quality variance will help managers make decision and plan their strategies in the competitive hospitality market environment.

Results and Discussions

The study has been based on three fragments namely customer expectation of service quality from star hotels, customer perception of service quality from star hotels and the gap between customer expectation and perception of service quality from star hotels Based on the analysis done we take each of the 50 potential factors, and segregate them under ten broad criteria namely **Presentation, Facilities of the Hotel, Hotel Front Office, Room Product, Food & Beverage Service, Food and Beverage production, Personalised Service, Service In General Hotel Staff and overall service quality.**

Presentation

During the analysis it was found that the there was no significant difference between service quality expectations related to Presentation of Chain Hotels and Standalone Hotels. The guests expects the same kind of presentation including the ambience, style etc. the guest have perceived both the hotels equally and also it was found that is no significant difference in service quality gaps (Customer Expected - Customer Perceived) relating to Presentation of Chain Hotels and Standalone Hotels

Facilities of the Hotel

In the study it was found that there is no significant difference between service quality expectations related to Facilities of Chain Hotels and Standalone Hotels. But there was a significant difference between service quality perceptions related to Facilities of Chain Hotels and Standalone Hotels.

When we looked into the Chain Hotels scored less than Standalone Hotels in giving **"Fabulous views from the hotel room"**, The Standalone hotel have to attract customers based on their location. Hence they give more attention to the view from the rooms. They understand the importance of retaining the customer. According to a research by Reichheld and Sasser in the Harvard Business Review, 5 per cent increase in customer retention can increase profitability by 35 per cent in hoteliering business, 50 per cent in insurance and brokerage, and 125 per cent in the consumer credit card market.

In the **"Timesaving services such as valet parking"** Chain hotels as well as standalone hotels have scored equally in this criterion and take initiatives in providing customers with good valet parking service. A good valet parking facility not only impress in house guest but also make an impression on people coming from outside like for banquet functions etc. the hotels have realized the importance of the same and so pay importance to it

When we see **"Floor concierge"**, Standalone hotels have scored better than Chain hotels. In hotels, a concierge assists guests with various tasks like making restaurant reservations, arranging for spa services, recommending night life hot spots, booking transportation (limousines, airplanes, boats, etc.), procurement of tickets to special events and assisting with various travel arrangements and tours of local attractions. In upscale establishments, a concierge is often expected to "achieve the impossible", dealing with any request a guest may have, no matter how strange, relying on an extensive list of contacts with local merchants and service providers. Concierge is a personalized service and the research show that Standalone hotels pay more attention on concierge service

In "**Provision of gym and other recreational facilities**" Chain hotels have scored better than Standalone hotels. Chain hotels generally sign up with fitness companies to man their gym so the facility and quality of their gym is very high as compared to standalone properties who are not able to do the same

In the criteria **"Shops within the hotel"** Chain hotels have scored better than Standalone hotels. We can see a remarkable difference in the score of hotels this may be because generally Chain hotels sign up with big retail brands to open shops on their premises in all their Chain properties where as the Standalone properties find it difficult to do so as they have only one property and the retailers don't find it profitable. Thus the number of shops in a standalone property is very less as compared to Chain hotels.

In **"High level of security"** Standalone hotels have scored better than Chain hotels. Security has become a major concern of the hotels especially after the terrorist attack on Mumbai hotels. The research shows that the security levels in standalone properties are better. The reason is that being individual property it is easier to keep a track on guest and employees than Chain hotels as the numbers are limited and also the procedures and policies of the hotels can be molded to the need of the property

In the **"Overall Facilities of the Hotel"** Chain hotels have scored better than Standalone hotels. Overall guests have perceived Chain hotels better than Standalone hotels as they give a better impression as far as facilities is concerned.

But when we study the gap both Chain Hotels and Standalone Hotels have failed to meet the customer's expectation in most of the sub-elements of Facilities in the Hotel. The modern guest expects a lot as far as facilities of the hotels is concerned. The customer expects an overall package from the hotel wherein the hotel should have a good view, a good valet parking, and recreational facility and with all this a high level of security. The above gap reflects that both Chain Hotels and Standalone hotels do not provide apt facilities expected by the guest. Only in providing shops within the Hotel standalone hotels have exceeded the expectation of the guest by providing shops on premises for guest use. The Hotels need to work a lot as far as facilities are concerned as the gap between expectation of the guest and perception of the guest is very high.

Hotel Front Office

During the study it was revealed that there is a significant difference between service quality expectation related to Hotel front office of Standalone and Chain Hotels

If we compare the services expectation of guest from front office of Chain Hotels as compared with Standalone hotels, the service expectation is much higher from chain Hotels. In different criteria of front office such as "**check-in check-out process, "billing accuracy", "Airport services"** etc. guest expect better service from chain hotels than Standalone Hotels.

But there is a significant difference between service quality perceptions related to Hotel front office of Standalone and Chain Hotels. If we compare the services provided by the front office of Chain hotels and Standalone Hotels, Standalone hotels have been perceived much better as compared to Chain Hotels like in the criteria "**Check in & check out process**" Standalone hotels have scored better than Chain hotels. In the criteria "**Travel desk service** "again the Standalone hotels have scored better. Also in "**Billing accuracy**" Standalone hotels have a better scoring over Chain Hotels. In the "**Bell desk service**" both the categories of hotels have scored equivalent. The guest has perceived both equally well.

In the only criteria where Chain Hotels have done well is "**Airport service offered by the Hotel**" where Chain hotels have scored better than Standalone hotels. The guest has perceived the airport services of Chain Hotels to be better than Standalone.

If we see the "**Overall**" scoring of front office services of Chain Hotels and Standalone hotels, Chain hotels have performed poor or the guest have perceived Standalone hotels better

When we see the gap we summarize that Front office is the face of the hotel and it is very important that the Hotel front office is good as it creates the first impression of the hotel on the guests. Both Chain Hotels and Standalone Hotels have failed to meet the guest's expectation in all the sub-elements of Hotel Front Office. It is relevant from the table that both the Chain Hotels as well as Standalone Hotels need to pay more attention to their front office operations so as to exceed guest expectations. The expectation from chain hotels is higher so they need to work even hard to exceed guest expectations

Room Product

During the study it was revealed that there is a significant difference between service quality expectations related to Room Product of Standalone and Chain Hotels.

The expectation of guest as far as room product goes is higher from Chain Hotels than Standalone hotels. In providing **"Large, comfortable beds", "Linen quality", "Range of toiletries available in the bathroom"** expectation from chain Hotel is higher. The guest also expects better range of toiletries in Chain hotels than in standalone Hotels. In providing **"Provision of stationery in the room"** Chain hotels have scored better than Standalone hotels. In providing stationeries Chain hotels are expected to provide more number and better stationeries than Standalone hotels like personalized stationary with guest name written on the letter head etc. The guest expectation in providing **"Spacious room and bathrooms"** also Chain hotels have scored better. Large rooms and bathroom with ample amenities is what the guest expects from Chain hotels. Overall chain hotels are expected to have better room product as compared to standalone hotels. This indicates that the guest expectation from Chain hotels is very high as far as room products are concerned. The only criteria where the Standalone hotels are expected better are in providing **"Large, comfortable beds"** and **"Luxurious branded toiletries"** where Standalone hotels have scored better. Today's clientele is brand conscious and thus expects hotels to have branded amenities in the rooms.

When the guest perception was measured it was found that there was significant difference between service quality perceptions related to Room Product of Standalone and Chain Hotels.

In providing **"Large, comfortable beds"** Standalone hotels have been perceived better than Chain hotels. Their quality of bed have been perceived better by the guest as the quality of both mattress and bed is extremely good

In the criteria **"Luxurious branded toiletries"** Standalone hotels have scored better. The quality of branded toiletries provided by the Standalone hotels is much better than the Chain hotels. Chain hotels generally concentrate more on quantity and miss out on quality.

In providing **"Linen quality"** Standalone hotels have scored better. The number of towels as well as the quality of linen as compared to the Chain hotels, the Standalone hotels has been perceived better.

In the criteria **"Range of toiletries available in the bathroom", "Spacious room and bathrooms"** Standalone hotels have scored better.

When we see **"Provision of stationery in the room"** Chain hotels have scored better. The reason being the personalized stationeries being used by Chain hotels which includes letter head with the guest name written etc. which is highly appreciated by the guest.

In keeping **"Deluxe appliances"** Chain hotels have scored extremely high. The reason here is that the Chain hotels generally sign up with good brand to supply appliances for all their hotels at a cheap rate which the Standalone properties are unable to do, so they are not able to afford the appliances to be put in the rooms.

The expectation from chain hotels in room product is very high from chain hotels but the guests have perceived standalone hotels better.

If we see the overall score Standalone hotels have scored better than Chain hotels. The reason being that Standalone properties are able to concentrate more on individual need of the clientele and most of their suppliers are local, so they do not run short on supplies. They have pillow menus to provide variety of pillows and also for toiletries they are able to easily change them according to the season or need of the customer.

It is suggested that the chain Hotels should pay more attention to their room product. Rooms fetch more than fifty percent of total revenues earned by the hotels, so it is up most important that the hotels provide the best of the products in terms of quality and quantity in the rooms. Most of the chain hotels have centralized purchasing where one head office Hotel purchases guest amenities for the entire chain. Sometimes they are not able to meet the expectation of clients of different regions, so the Chain Hotels should also look at supplying local stuff. With that they will have enough stock and also be able to meet the expectation of the guests

Food & Beverage Service

In the study it was found that there is no significant difference between service quality expectations related to Food & Beverage Service of Standalone and Chain Hotels. The guest expects the same kind of service from both the categories of hotel. But when the measurement for perception was done, it was found that there is a significant difference between service quality perception related to Food & Beverage Service of Standalone and Chain Hotels

In providing **"Provision of a sumptuous buffet"**, **"Good range of bars to buy a drink"**, **"Fairly priced food and beverage"**, **"Affordability of items in the mini bar"** Chain hotels have been perceived better than Standalone hotels. In **"Overall food and beverage service"** Chain hotels have scored better by getting a score better than Standalone hotels. This shows that in Chain Hotels provide bigger range of food and beverage products in restaurants, bars and minibar, and with better pricing whereas if we see the providing **"Staff knowledge of menu"** , **"Quality of service"**,

"Economical items available for room service" where Standalone hotels have been perceived better

The scores show that where the Chain hotels have scored well in proving better variety of Food and Beverage Service, in the same place Standalone hotels have done extremely well in giving good food quality and staff knowledge of food. Both categories of hotels have showed their strong sides where the Chain hotels are concentrating more in variety and Standalone concentrate more on quality of food and beverage.

It is suggested that the standalone Hotels should also concentrate on variety and Chain hotels should concentrate more on quality of food and beverage to exceed guest expectation.

Food and Beverage production

During the study it was found that there was a significant difference between service quality expectations related to Food & Beverage Product of Standalone and Chain Hotels.

In providing **"Quality of food"**, **"Taste of food"** the guest's expectation from Standalone hotels is much higher than Chain Hotels. In the criteria **"Portion size of dishes"** again the guest has expected Standalone Hotels to give better portion size. In providing **"Provision of live counters"** guest expectation from Chain hotels is higher. The guest expects more live counter in Chain hotels than in Standalone hotels. Also in **"Exquisite food presentation"** the guest expectation from Chain hotels is high. If we see **"Overall"** expectation as far as food and beverage product is concerned, form Standalone hotels are much higher as compared to Chain Hotels.

It was also relevant during the study that there was no significant difference between service quality perceptions related to Food & Beverage Product of Standalone and Chain Hotels. The guests of both categories of hotels perceived the hotels equally

As we can see from the table above, the gap between food and beverage product expected and perceived by the guest in chain hotels is higher than Standalone Hotels, whether it was Quality of food, Exquisite food presentation, Taste of food, Portion size of dishes or Provision of live counters chain hotels have not come up to the expectation of the guest. Even the standalone hotels have failed in meeting guest expectations.

Food and beverage product of any Hotel is the key to its success. It is suggested that both Standalone and Chain Hotel should pay more attention to the food products being offered to the guest. The food offered to the guest not only attract in-house guest but also visitors who come to the restaurant or come for banqueting, which again adds to the total revenue earned by the Hotel. It is very important and crucial that the hotels should serve best quality food and good variety of food to their guest.

Personalised Service

From the study it was found that there was a significant difference between service quality expectations related to Personalised Service of Standalone and Chain Hotels.

The expectation of guest as far as Personalised service goes is higher from Chain Hotels than Standalone hotels. In providing **"Guest relation service"** ," **To be acknowledged rather than to be treated as just another customer"**, "**To be made to feel special"**, "**Staff remembering your requirements"**, "**The staff remember your name"** Chain hotels have scored better than Standalone hotels.. All the above score clearly indicates that the guest expectation of personalized service from Chain hotels is extremely high. Considering the fact that even when we see the overall score Chain hotels have scored better than Standalone hotels. The difference in the score is big and is a clear indication of the service expectation of the guests from the Hotels. The guests expect the Chain hotels to be more standardized and staff being more professional in handling guests services.

It was also found that there was a significant difference between service quality perceptions related to Personalised Service of Standalone and Chain Hotels.

In providing "**Guest relation service**", "**To be acknowledged rather than to be treated as just another customer**", "**To be made to feel special**" Standalone hotels have scored better than Chain hotels. **"Overall"** Standalone hotels have scored better than Chain hotels in the above mentioned criteria. Whereas in providing "**Staff remembering your requirements**", **The staff remember your name**" Chain hotels have scored better.

This gives a clear picture that in providing personalized service guest perceives that Standalone hotels do a better job. A reason for this might be that the staff is well trained in performing their job. But when we see other criteria like "**Staff remembering your requirements**" and "**The staff remember your name**" Chain hotels have taken the lead. The reason for this might be that Chain hotels generally have very good software which has a function called "guest history", where the staff fills in the details of guest likes and dislikes so that it can be remembered on his next visit. The same way the telephones also reflect the guest name when the guest call from rooms, so whoever picks up the calls can address guest by name.

It is suggested that staff training should be taken very seriously. In giving excellent personalized service training plays a very important role. Hotels should have constructive training classes and also they should have a good software with caller ID to recognize guest name and room number etc.

Service In General

In the study it was revealed that there is a significant difference between service quality expectations related to Service In General of Standalone and Chain Hotels. In providing **"Not being kept waiting for more than a minute"**, **"Immediate service"**, **"Professional service"** Chain hotels are expected to be better. But if we see the criteria **"Every need is anticipated"**, **"Precise attention to detail"** Standalone hotels are expected to be better .The expectation of guest about service in general from Chain Hotels as well as Standalone Hotels is similar. In few categories like Not being kept waiting for more than a minute, Immediate service and Professional service, the guest expectations from Chain hotels is higher whereas in criteria's like Every need is anticipated and Precise attention to detail, the expectations of guest from Standalone hotels is higher. But overall the guests expect better service from Chain Hotels than Standalone Hotels. The reason might be the overall impression of the guests about the Chain properties or the experience in other properties of same Chain.

In the study it was also revealed that there is a significant difference between service quality perceptions related to Service In General of Standalone and Chain Hotels. In providing **"Not being kept waiting for more than a minute"**, **"Every need is anticipated"**, **"Precise attention to detail"** Standalone hotels have scored better than chain hotels i.e. the guest have perceived standalone hotels better than chain hotels. In providing **"Immediate service"**, **"Professional service"** Chain hotels have been perceived better than Standalone hotels But if we see **"Overall"** Chain hotels have been perceived better than Standalone hotels.

Here we can see a big difference in the guest perception of service in general between Chain hotels and Standalone hotels. The guest perceives that the Chain hotels give immediate and professional service as compared to Standalone hotels. The reason for the same can be better training of staff and better use of technology

It is relevant from the study that both Chain hotels and Standalone Hotels have failed in meeting guest expectations in providing service in general. The Gap between expected and perceived service quality is more in Standalone hotels as compared to Chain Hotels. This clearly indicates that as far as service in general is concerned the standalone Hotels need to pay more attention to details, give more professional and speedy service. As far as chain Hotels are concerned they need to pay more attention to anticipate guest need rather than the guest waiting for it. Today's guests are busy and have no time for waiting for any services and if the hotels want to excel themselves to other hotels they will have to focus more on speedy, accurate service with attention to detail.

Hotel Staff

The study revealed that there is a significant difference between service quality expectations related to Hotel staff of Standalone and Chain Hotels.

In providing **"Staff who understand and meet unusual requests"**, **"Smiling and friendly staff"**, **"Staff who anticipate your needs"** , **"Staff who understand classy patrons"** Chain hotels have scored better than Standalone hotels. When we look at **"Overall"** scores Chain hotels are expected to be much better in providing quality staff than Standalone hotels.

The scores clearly indicate that the expectation of Hotel staff from Chain hotels as compared to Standalone Hotels is very high. The guest expects that the staff of Chain hotels is well trained. The staff should be able to understand the guest needs. They should be friendly and polished. Rather than the guest asking for service the staff should be able to anticipate their need. The staff should be able to understand the type of guest like business or family and also the strata they come from and the staff should treat the guest with that. The expectations from the guest about the staff of Chain hotels comprise of all these qualities and are extremely high as compared to Standalone properties.

The study also revealed that there is a significant difference between service quality perceptions related to Hotel staff of Standalone and Chain Hotels.

In providing "**Staff who understand and meet unusual requests**", "**Smiling and friendly staff**" "**Staff who anticipate your needs**" Chain hotels have been perceived better than Standalone hotels. Whereas in providing "**High quality staff who are well trained**", "**Staff who understand classy patrons**" Standalone hotels have been perceived better than Chain Hotels. "**Overall**" Chain hotels have been perceived better than Standalone hotels. It clearly indicates that as far as Hotel staff is concerned Chain hotels have been perceived better by guests. This criterion highlights the training capabilities of a hotel where the Chain hotels have surpassed the Standalone hotels.

The Gap between expected and perceived service quality is more in Chain Hotels than Standalone Hotels. Hotel industry is a service industry and the services are rendered by staff. Overall if we look at the figures it clearly indicates that the hotels have failed in meeting guest expectation as far as staff is concerned. One of the prime reasons of this can be the high turnover of staff in the Hotel industry and also lack of skilled labour. Training also plays a key role as far as staff performance is concerned. The hotel industry altogether is lagging in providing good, professional and trained staff to deliver better service.

It is suggested that the Hotels should give importance to hire staff with right qualification and right attitude to serve guests. Ongoing training is mandatory and will definitely help staff to perform better. Hotels should work on staff welfare program and other motivational aspects to reduce on employee turnover.

Overall service quality

The study revealed that there is no significant difference between service quality expectations related to overall service quality of Standalone and Chain Hotels. The guest expects the same quality service as compared to a chain hotel to a standalone Hotel

The study also revealed that there is a significant difference between service quality perceptions related to overall service quality of Standalone and Chain Hotels.

In providing **"Facilities of the Hotel"**, **"Food & Beverage service"**, **"Hotel Staff"** Chain hotels are perceived better than Standalone Hotels. Whereas in providing **"Presentation"**, **"Room Product"**, **"Personalised Service"**, **"Food & Beverage Product"**, **"Hotel Front office"** Standalone hotels are perceived to be better than Chain hotels.

When we see **"Overall Hotel"** Standalone hotels have scored better by getting a higher score than Chain hotels. Overall the guests have perceived Standalone hotels better than Chain hotels. Standalone hotels pay more attention to location of the hotel also their presentation is better perceived than Chain hotel. Their rooms and amenities are much better and also they are able to give much personalized service. The front office facilities and the food product are perceived much better by guest than as compared to Chain Hotels.

The study indicates that there is a major gap between service expectation and service perceived in both chain and standalone hotels.

In the study it was also very relevant that the guest expectations from the chain hotels are much higher than the guest expectations from standalone hotels. Thus for standalone hotels to meet guest expectation is easier than chain hotels. But overall both the type of hotels has not met 100% guest expectation and so they need to work a lot on meeting and exceeding guest expectation.

Ongoing structured training and standard operating procedures can help the hotels a lot to be more organized, improve their quality and exceed guest expectations

Limitations

There are a number of limitations recognised within this research. The limitations relate to the data sample and the range of variables contained within the research model.

The research gained a substantial respondent sample within the Indian star hotel sectors. The data were gathered from five hotels located within Bangalore. The limitations of this research related to the data collection approach whereby the hotels are of a limited number, are all located within one state of Karnataka and are within a limited range of hotel standards.

In addition to the limited sampling framework a further limitation is associated with the use of self-completion survey methods. Although survey research is the most widely used approach in the world (Neuman, 2003) there are a number of problems associated. The lack of researcher control in a self completion process necessitates that the resultant data sample will not be fully representative of the population as valid respondents may choose not to complete the survey. There are also limitations associated with survey completion with respondents sometimes giving expected answers or pattern responses to questions.

The third area of limitations relates to the variables contained within the research model. Although the research model contains the dimensions that are central to the research question around which this thesis has been constructed there are a number of possible other dimensions that could also affect the relationships that flow between hotel performance

The inclusion of questions related to respondents frequency and experience of hotel consumption would have enabled evaluation of the impact of these on the variables. A further area of limitations relates to the constraints adopted of studying star hotels together. Although these sections of the hotel industry exhibit a number of similarities that encourage their combined study, the sectors are distinct. The distinctions were evident in aspects of the qualitative research, in which some noticeable differences of expectations were evident between star consumers. This research was unable to fully explore these distinctions, as they were extraneous to the research question.

Scope for future work

There are a number of opportunities for future research that reflects the limitations recognised above. Firstly the limitations recognised in relation to the data collection provide opportunities for future research. The research could be replicated in other geographic locations. Extending this research into the European, Asian and American contexts would provide opportunity to address the impact of cultural background, including the effect of collectivism and individualism, on the research model. Equally the chain and standalone hotel sectors are only a two of the recognised hotel standards and replication of this research within the economy and mid-price sectors would be valuable. The application of the final survey instrument in other countries would allow the robustness of the developed scales to be ascertained.

Secondly as recognised above there are a number of other dimensions that could be included in the research model and it is recommended that the research be replicated with the addition of further dimensions to further the understanding of the relationships that affect hotel service quality. Thirdly, an opportunity for future research lies in the study of the difference in expectations between consumers of Chain hotels and stand alone hotels identified from the qualitative study. The distinctions identified between expectations of Chain hotels and stand alone hotels consumers present a number of research opportunities relating to comparative satisfaction of these different consumer groups with their hotel experience. The differences between the Chain hotels and stand alone hotels also need further research in relation to the other constructs included in this research.

Finally the research identifies a number of aspects that may be applicable within the wider service sector and these aspects need to be tested in other industries. For example this research has confirmed that service quality is a higher order construct with the Chain hotels and stand alone hotels of the hotel industry but there would be benefits from replicating this in other service industries. Other relationships identified in this research also need to be tested in a range of other service industries.

CHAPTER 1.6
APPENDIX

HOTEL CONSUMPTION QUESTIONNAIRE

The (Hotel Name) Hotel and the M.S.Ramaiah College of Hotel Management at Bangalore are jointly working together to study consumer expectations of hotels and specifically how this hotel meets your expectations.

As an incentive to complete the questionnaire there will be a draw for a prize of a short break (two nights accommodation) at the (Hotel Name Deleted) Hotel generously donated by them. Please complete your name and contact phone number on the enclosed questionnaire.

I would like to emphasize that this survey is anonymous. You do not need to write your name or any other information which can identify you on the survey. The prize holiday would be offered only to the guest who writes their detail and their detail will only be accessed to identify the winner of the draw.

Once you have completed the questionnaire could you please return it to the reception. If you have any questions or suggestions, please feel free to contact me (Ms. Malini Singh) on telephone (09449052326) or by email on malinisingh27@gmail.com

Thank you; please continue by completing the questionnaire.

Yours truly,
Malini Singh

Personal Details

Name-

Age - Tick the appropriate age group

20 – 30 years

31 – 40 years

41 – 50 years

More than 51 years.

Income- Tick the appropriate income group

Less than Rs. 4 lakhs per annum

Rs. 4 lakhs to Rs. 6 lakhs

More than Rs. 6 lakhs per annum

Purpose of visit- Tick the appropriate purpose of visit

Business

Leisure

Other

Contact number/email id

Room no.

(Name Deleted) hotel. Please rate the extent to which you think the hotel possessed the features described by each statement.

Column 1 Importance

Please rate how **important** it is to you that the hotel possesses the characteristics of each item described below.

Please write a score in this column from

1.. 5...

10

| Not at all | Moderately | Extremely |
| important | important | Important |

Column 2 Performance

Please rate how **effective** the hotel was in delivering each item described below. Please write a score in this column from

1... 5...

10

| Very | Moderately | Very |
| Poor | effective | Good |

Presentation of Hotel	Importance to me of each item in relation to hotel choice 1 to 10	Performance of hotel in relation to each item 1 to 10
1. The presentation of the hotel is professional		
2. The hotel is exclusive		
3. The ambience of the hotel is relaxing		
4. The hotel atmosphere is stylish		
5. The hotel is first class		

	Significantly below my expectations	Moderately below my expectations	Met my expectations	Moderately above my expectations	Signiy above expec
To what extent did the '*overall presentation*' of the hotel compare with the expectations you held prior to arriving at the hotel?	1	2	3	4	5

Facilities of the Hotel	**Importance to me** of each item in relation to hotel choice 1 to 10	**Performance** of hotel in relation to each item 1 to 10
1. Fabulous views from the hotel room		
2. Timesaving services such as valet parking		
3. Floor concierge		
4. Provision of gym and other recreational facilities		
5. Shops within the hotel		
6. High level of security		

	Significantly below my expectations	Moderately below my expectation	Met my expectations	Moderately above my expectations	Significantly above my expectations
To what extent did the above mentioned features of the *'Facilities of the hotel'* compare with the expectations you held prior to arriving at the hotel?	1	2	3	4	5

Hotel Front Office	Importance to me of each item in relation to hotel choice 1 to 10	Performance of hotel in relation to each item 1 to 10
1. Check in & check out process		
2. Bell desk service		
3.Travel desk service		
4. Billing accuracy		
5. Airport service offered by the Hotel		

	Significantly below my expectations	Moderately below my expectations	Met my expectations	Moderately above my expectations	Significantly above my expectations
To what extent did the *hotel front office* compare with the expectations you held prior to arriving at the hotel?	1	2	3	4	5

Room Product	Importance to me of each item in relation to hotel choice 1 to 10	Performance of hotel in relation to each item 1 to 10
1. Large, comfortable beds		
2. Luxurious branded toiletries		
3. Linen quality		
4. Range of toiletries available in the bathroom		
5. Provision of stationery in the room		
6. Spacious room and bathrooms		
7. Deluxe appliances		

	Significantly below my expectations	Moderately below my expectations	Met my expectations	Moderately above my expectations	Significantly above my expectations
To what extent did the overall 'room product' compare with the expectations you held prior to arriving at the hotel?	1	2	3	4	5

Food & Beverage service	Importance to me of each item in relation to hotel choice 1 to 10	Performance of hotel in relation to each item 1 to 10
1. Provision of a sumptuous buffet		
2. Good range of bars to buy a drink		
3. Staff knowledge of menu		
4. Quality of service		
5. Fairly priced food and beverage		
6. Economical items available for room service		
7. Affordability of items in the mini bar		

	Significantly below my expectations	Moderately below my expectations	Met my expectations	Moderately above my expectations	Significantly above my expectations
To what extent did the overall *'food and beverage service'* compare with the expectations you held prior to arriving at the hotel?	1	2	3	4	5

Food and Beverage Production	**Importance to me** of each item in relation to hotel choice 1 to 10	**Performance** of hotel in relation to each item 1 to 10
1. Quality of food		
2. Exquisite food presentation		
3. Taste of food		
4. Portion size of dishes		
5. Provision of live counters		

	Significantly below my expectations	Moderately below my expectations	Met my expectations	Moderately above my expectations	Significantly above my expectations
To what extent did the (Hotel Name Deleted) Hotel give you "food and Beverage Product" compared with the expectations you held prior to arriving at the hotel?	1	2	3	4	5

Personalized Service	Importance to me of each item in relation to hotel choice 1 to 10	Performance of hotel in relation to each item 1 to 10
1. Guest relation service		
2. To be acknowledged rather than to be treated as just another customer		
3. To be made to feel special		
4. Staff remembering your requirements		
5. The staff remember your name		

	Significantly below my expectations	Moderately below my expectations	Met my expectations	Moderately above my expectations	Significantly above my expectations
To what extent did the 'personalized' service' aspect compare with the expectations you held prior to arriving at the hotel ?	1	2	3	4	5

Service in General	**Importance to me** of each item in relation to hotel choice 1 to 10	**Performance** of hotel in relation to each item 1 to 10
1. Not being kept waiting for more than a minute		
2. Immediate service		
3. Every need is anticipated		
4. Precise attention to detail		
5. Professional service		

	Signific antly below my expectat ions	Moderately below my expectations	Met my expectations	Moderately above my expectations	Significantly above my expectations
To what extent did the *overall service performance* compare with the expectations you held prior to arriving at the hotel?	1	2	3	4	5

Hotel Staff	**Importance to me** of each item in relation to hotel choice 1 to 10	**Performance** of hotel in relation to each item 1 to 10
1. Staff who understand and meet unusual requests		
2. High quality staff who are well trained		
3. Smiling and friendly staff		
4. Staff who anticipate your needs		
5. Staff who understand classy patrons		

	Significantly below my expectations	Moderately below my expectations	Met my expectations	Moderately above my expectations	Significantly above my expectations
To what extent did the 'hotel staff' compare with the expectations you held prior to arriving at the hotel?	1	2	3	4	5